P U B W

I

West Essex

Norman Skinner

COUNTRYSIDE BOOKS
NEWBURY, BERKSHIRE

First Published 1995
© Norman Skinner 1995

COUNTRYSIDE BOOKS
3 Catherine Road
Newbury, Berkshire

ISBN 1 85306 338 X

Designed by Mon Mohan
Cover illustration by Colin Doggett
Maps and photographs by Ann Skinner

Produced through MRM Associates Ltd., Reading
Typeset by The Midlands Book Typesetting Company, Loughborough
Printed by J.W. Arrowsmith Ltd., Bristol

Contents

Introduction   6

Walk 1   Debden: The White Hart (3³/₄ miles)   8

2   Wicken Bonhunt: The Coach and Horses
(3¹/₂ miles)   13

3   Clavering: The Fox and Hounds (3¹/₂ miles)   18

4   Molehill Green: The Three Horseshoes
(4 miles)   22

5   Great Hallingbury: The Hop Poles (3 miles)   26

6   Little Dunmow: The Flitch of Bacon
(3¹/₄ miles)   31

7   Hatfield Broad Oak: The Cock (5 miles)   35

8   Matching Tye: The Fox (3¹/₂ miles)   40

9   Great Waltham: The Beehive (4 miles)   44

10   Nazeing: The King Harold's Head (4 miles)   48

11   Epping Green: The Travellers Friend
(4 miles)   52

12   Good Easter: ~~The Star~~ (4 miles)   58

(handwritten annotations: 4/5/08 beside Walk 8; 28/9/2003 beside Walk 10; 11/3/2007 beside Walk 11; 12/8/99 beside Walk 12; "Sine" written below Walk 12)

13 Stapleford Tawney: The Mole Trap (5 miles) 63

14 Stanford Rivers: The Drill House (3¼ miles) 67

15 Willingale: The Maltsters Arms (5¼ miles) 71

16 Radley Green: The Thatcher's Arms
    (6½ miles) 75

17 Edney Common: The Green Man (4 miles) 79

18 Theydon Bois: The Sixteen String Jack
    (6 miles) 83

19 Abridge: The Maltsters Arms (5 miles) 87

20 Navestock Heath: The Plough (6 miles) 92

Publisher's Note

We hope that you obtain considerable enjoyment from this book; great care has been taken in its preparation. However, changes of landlord and actual closures are sadly not uncommon. Likewise, although at the time of publication all routes followed public rights of way or permitted paths, diversion orders can be made and permissions withdrawn.

We cannot of course be held responsible for such diversion orders and any resultant inaccuracies in the text which result from these or any other changes to the routes nor any damage which might result from walkers trespassing on private property. We are anxious that all details covering the walks and the pubs are kept up to date and would therefore welcome information from readers which would be relevant to future editions.

① Debden
② Wicken Bonhunt
③ Clavering
④ Molehill Green
⑤ Great Hallingbury   ⑥ Little Dunmow
⑦ Hatfield Broad Oak
⑧ Matching Tye
⑨ Great Waltham
⑩ Nazeing   ⑪ Epping Green
⑫ Good Easter
Stapleford Tawney ⑬
⑮ Willingale
Theydon ⑱   ⑲ Abridge   ⑭ Stanford   ⑯   ⑰ Edney Common
Bois   Rivers   Radley Green
⑳ Navestock Heath

Area map showing locations of the walks.

Introduction

It is a remarkable fact that the pubs in this book, sometimes only a few miles from London, are largely unspoilt by metropolitanism, while the surrounding countryside of west Essex affords freedom and tranquillity to walk in often beautiful surroundings. On a fine day in the spring and summer many of us are tempted outdoors for a walk with friends. That each walk described in this book is based on one of our excellent Essex pubs probably provides an added incentive! Do not ignore the winter though, when the bright light reflected on the snow can be a delight, and autumn can be the finest time of all when the trees and bushes take on their spectacular colours.

The usual caveats apply. All these pubs are keen to serve you; however I have made individual notes on the subject of car parking and the reception given to children and dogs. What *is* a universal must is that mud should not be brought into the pub. The simple way round this is that after a walk you should either change your shoes, or remove them to just wear socks, or don covers over your footwear to protect carpets etc. This is what most walkers now do.

The pub as an institution has played its part in village life for many hundreds of years. A development which has become more widespread over the last 20 years has been the provision of snacks and meals. Though not at first universally welcomed, there are many who now enjoy this service. The standard of beer is also undoubtedly higher than pre-1970, the CAMRA organisation having obtained public support in promoting the demand and therefore the production of 'real ale'.

Footpaths in general must come in for some praise. We have still some way to go but the combination of the local authorities, the Ramblers' Association, and many of the landowners has effected great improvements on the Essex footpath network so that many more members of the public are out and about.

The directions, together with the sketch maps will enable you to find your way. If possible, in addition carry the OS Landranger map. All the walks are contained in map 167. If you possess a compass that too can be useful.

Once again I wish to express my gratitude to my wife Ann for providing all the maps and photographs. Without her encouragement and support the business of writing this book would have been much harder.

I have often been asked to confirm that researching these pub books must have been lots of fun. In truth it has been fascinating to learn more details of pubs which previously were known only casually, and to find routes not all of which I have previously walked. It has given me great pleasure to meet people who have taken up walking on a regular basis as a result of buying one of my Essex pub walks books. I do hope that this process will continue with this west Essex book. Perhaps I will meet you one fine day on the paths of Essex or in one of the country pubs we favour. 'Till then I wish you happy days walking in Essex.

Norman Skinner
Spring 1995

1 Debden
The White Hart

Debden is a beautiful village, with a rich collection of old houses and farms within the parish. The White Hart commands a central position opposite the school, with the church down the lane across from the village pond. A friendly welcome awaits you both from the landlord and his staff and also in my experience from local customers who comprise a lot of the trade.

Children are welcome. The real ales are simply Greene King IPA and Abbot Ale, the draught cider in the White Hart is Red Rock.

Pub opening hours are 11.30am – 3pm and 6pm – 11pm Mondays to Saturdays. On Sunday they are open 12 noon – 3pm and 7pm – 10.30pm. Food is served 12 noon – 2pm every day and 7pm – 10pm Tuesdays to Saturdays. On Sunday roast lunches are popular, but throughout the week there are tempting items from the menu, such as home-made soup, mini roast leg of lamb, steak and kidney pie, lamb balti, chicken curry and apple pie. All of these are home-made and to be enjoyed. Otherwise sandwiches or other snacks can be chosen. Dogs are not admitted.

Telephone: 01799 541109.

How to get there: Debden is on a minor road a few miles south of Saffron Walden. If coming along the B1383 from Stansted Mountfitchet, after about 4 miles this road crosses over the M11 and soon you turn right on to a road leading to Widdington. Before you get there turn left and follow the signs to Debden.

Parking: Park at the pub. If there is no room park at the village shop which is just before you reach the pond. If in the pub car park please ask permission to leave your car before setting out on the walk.

Length of the walk: 3³/₄ miles. OS Landranger map 167 Chelmsford and Harlow (GR 556334).

A beautiful walk with views from Swaynes Hall over the valley to Debden church and village. This is a lovely part of Essex and the source of the river Chelmer lies only a mile away at Rowney Wood, east of the White Hart. On the walk you pass close to Mole Hall wildlife reserve, and you may wish to follow your walk with a wander round the reserve (open 10.30am – 6pm Easter onwards, there is an admission fee).

The Walk

From the pub cross the road to a concrete public footpath signpost. Walk past a school with mobile classroom extensions and continue on a pebbly path and on with a ditch and hedge on your left. On your right in a hollow you can see the church tower.

Coming to a wood (Brocton's Plantation) bear left with the wood on your right. At the end of the wood carry straight on

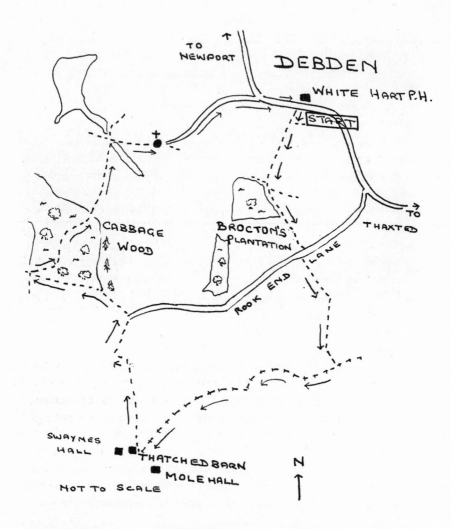

with a hedge on your left, walking downhill towards a sewage works. Keep left round the fence to a large bridge at the back. Turn left over the bridge by a public footpath signpost and cross over Rook End Lane and walk by a concrete public bridleway signpost. This is called Sampson's Lane. It is a well used track for horses and so at some times of the year it can be rather muddy. However, you can escape to the field edge above!

Debden church.

On reaching a small wood bear left for a few yards to a crossing track, turn right and continue between trees. Soon you come out to a larger open field. Carry on, on a track between fields. On reaching a hedge bear left with a hedge on your right and admire the wide views on your right.

Just before the hedge goes right, turn right through a gap with the hedge now on your left. At the field corner pass through a gap into a hedged lane. On reaching a thatched barn (part of the garden of Swaynes Hall) at a public footpath signpost turn right, following a hedge on your left round to the left. The Mole Hall wildlife reserve is nearby to the south and you may have heard some strange animal noises as you approached this area! Turn right with a tall hedge on your left.

Nearing two thatched cottages cross over a ditch and turn left. At the corner turn right. Just past the cottages turn left at a concrete public byway signpost, keeping the hedge on your left. Keep left of the wood and turn right along the edge of the field. This wood (Cabbage Wood) is a wealth of beech and oak trees. Just after a building turn sharp right through a kissing-gate. The sign says 'Footpath only no cycles or horses'. Walk through this broad track admiring the varieties of trees present.

After leaving the wood continue on a track downhill passing a footpath sign on the left. Cross over a bridge with pools to the left and right. Immediately turn right along a narrow path. A large stone on your left is thought to be a pudding-stone.

Negotiate a stile and kissing-gate to enter the churchyard. The church is worth inspection. It is unusual in being built on lower lying land. St Mary the Virgin and All Saints is in a perfect setting. It has seen many changes, with a new chancel and bell turret in the 18th century. However, there is a 14th century doorway with 13th century arcades. One of the aisles is 14th century, the other a hundred years younger. There is a Tudor chest bound with iron, and an elaborate modern altar tomb to Trench Chiswell who rebuilt the chancel after it had been destroyed by the falling of the old tower. From the church walk up the road passing houses to left and right and arrive at the road right opposite the White Hart.

2 Wicken Bonhunt
The Coach and Horses

This delightful thatched rural pub is a Greene King house, not so frequently to be found on the west side of Essex, and it continues to be run with a friendly welcome both for locals and visitors. The building is about 300 years old and prior to opening as a pub in 1897 it was a blacksmith's forge. The church of St Margaret stands behind the pub and the land rises from the road on both sides, giving the village a sheltered feeling. The pub sign shows, in the coach, the faces of village characters past and present taken from cartoon sketches by Gill Potter.

The real ales are Greene King IPA and Abbot Ale and Rayments Special, while there is Red Rock and Dry Blackthorn cider on tap. A comprehensive selection of food is offered, ranging from sandwiches, ploughman's and jacket potatoes to steaks, grills and burgers etc (lunchtime only). Some dishes from the east include Balinese chicken, chicken tikka masala, and chicken Kiev, while the specials of the week are shown on the blackboard.

Food is served lunchtimes 12 noon – 2.30pm and evenings Monday to Saturday only 6.30pm – 9.30pm. You may wish to reserve. The pub opening hours are lunchtime Sunday to Friday 12 noon – 3pm, and evenings Monday to Friday 6pm – 11pm, Sunday 7pm – 10.30pm. On Saturdays the Coach and Horses is open 11am – 11pm. Children are welcome in the restaurant. Well behaved dogs can be taken into the public bar.

Telephone: 01799 540516.

How to get there: Wicken Bonhunt is a village on the B1038, south-west of Saffron Walden. The Coach and Horses is on the right if coming into the village from the Newport direction.

Parking: Park at the pub. Before setting out on your walk please ask the landlord's permission to leave your car.

Length of the walk: 3½ miles. OS Landranger map 167 Chelmsford and Harlow (GR 499333).

A magnificent short walk soon climbing to higher ground and views of Clavering to the west and Newport church to the east. The parish of Wicken Bonhunt is based on two hamlets: Wicken is the main part and follows the road and the stream Wicken Water, while Bonhunt is ³/₄ mile to the east and comprises a tiny Saxon chapel and three houses, one of which was a farm. In the course of the walk you visit Bonhunt, and the nearby hamlet and church of Rickling.

The Walk

From the Coach and Horses cross the road to a concrete public footpath signpost. Wicken is a streamside village, and just south of the main street Wicken Water runs west-east into the river Cam or Granta. You will encounter it again on the walk but for now cross over by a bridge and follow the path uphill between two gardens out into a field with a hedge on your

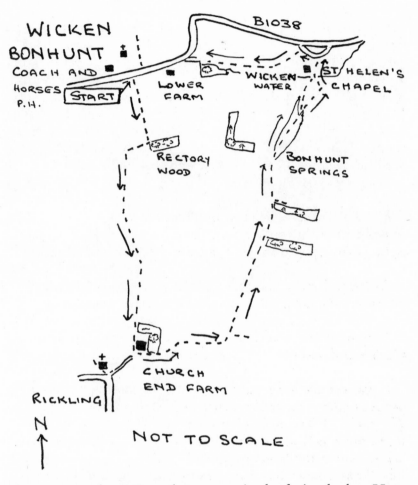

WICKEN
BONHUNT
COACH AND
HORSES
P.H.

START

LOWER FARM

B1038

WICKEN WATER

ST HELEN'S CHAPEL

RECTORY WOOD

BONHUNT SPRINGS

CHURCH END FARM

RICKLING

N

NOT TO SCALE

left. Continue for 300 yards to a gap in the facing hedge. Here turn right along the hedge, then turn left at the field corner and pass through a gap in the right-hand hedge. Again walk uphill with the hedge on your left, following the hedge round left-hand and right-hand turns.

In this short time you have climbed 100 feet from leaving the pub and the views are extensive all around. Continue on this splendid track and after ¾ mile arrive at Church End Farm at Rickling. Here are only two or three little thatched cottages keeping the company of a church mostly built in the

St Margaret's church, Wicken Bonhunt.

14th century but the foundation may be Saxon, and the nave is said to be 13th century.

If you have strayed from the farm to admire the church and buildings, make your way back to a concrete public bridleway signpost pointing east and follow a track with the farmhouse on your left. After 500 yards turn left ignoring a right turn and continue slowly downhill passing two small woods. You pass an area called Bonhunt Springs (the spring itself is to the west of the footpath and not visible) then turn left to cross a bridge over Wicken Water to arrive at St Helen's chapel. This is by far the oldest building in the district; used for many years as a barn it was a Saxon chapel, part of the Domesday hamlet Banhunta.

On reaching a road turn left for a few yards and then left again off it, following a path between fields back to pass a hedge end on your right and follow the Wicken Water and a hedge on your left. Follow this path for barely ½ mile passing a water treatment plant and a house, on to the road, the B1038.

Now you can walk past Wicken Hall (the Elizabethan manor house currently used as a study centre) and back to the pub, or you could take a look around Wicken itself.

St Margaret's church was virtually rebuilt in 1858 when it had fallen into a ruinous state, but the chancel is 13th century and there is an ancient scratch dial and piscina. The chancel has also kept some of its lancet windows, a small seat for the priest, and a monument to John Bradbury who died in 1693. He lived a few hundred yards away at Brick House, a handsome Tudor building with two fine gables and a 17th century thatched barn which has recently been converted into a private house.

Probably at the time of the church restoration the ancient custom of the curfew was reintroduced – the nightly ringing of the eight o'clock bell to remind villagers that bedtime was drawing near. This continued until the 1960s (with a break during the Second World War) when it was abandoned because no one could be found to replace the retiring verger. The village bakery, which used real wood-fired ovens, closed about the same time. A thriving signwriting business has taken over the premises.

After your visit to the church, it is only a short walk back to your car at the Coach and Horses.

3 Clavering
The Fox and Hounds

The Fox and Hounds has been considerably extended but it is still an attractive pub by any standards. Frank Dawes (author of *Afoot in Essex*, 1970) described it thus: 'a lovely picture confronted me framed by the old timber framed and weatherboarded inn with rambler roses round the porch and a lovely bank of garden flowers flanking the opposite side of the road'. A local book society met in the Fox and Hounds from 1787 to 1933.

The real ales are Greene King IPA, Abbot Ale, and Rayments Special bitter. A good selection of food includes soup of the day, egg mayonnaise, pâté, steak and mushroom pie, chilli and rice, lasagne, scampi, plaice, cod, skate (sometimes), salads, sandwiches and jacket potatoes. On Sundays there is always a roast meal available. Dogs are not allowed inside the bar; children are welcome providing they are well behaved. Opening hours are Monday to Saturday 12 noon – 2.30pm and

6pm – 11pm, Sundays 12 noon – 3pm and 7pm – 10.30pm.
Telephone: 01799 550321.

How to get there: Clavering is on the B1038 between Newport and Buntingford. From the direction of Newport, the Fox and Hounds is on the left in Clavering village.

Parking: Park at the pub car park at the rear. Please ask the landlord for permission to leave your car while you walk.

Length of the walk: 3½ miles. OS Landranger map 167 Chelmsford and Harlow (GR 476319).

It was in Clavering that Robert Fitz Wymarc built one of the first Norman castles in England, actually built before the Conquest. It made Clavering a place of importance in the Middle Ages. Now the walls have all gone leaving an extensive system of earthworks around the square moated compound where the castle stood. The old parts of the village are grouped about the castle site, so the castle which created the village still determines its layout.

The walk begins with a gentle stroll along the beautiful Stort valley then gives wide views as you climb towards Moat Farm. On the walk back enjoy identifying parts of historic Clavering as you descend.

The Walk

As you leave the Fox and Hounds turn left and left again to join the little lane with a no through road sign running south-east with the infant river Stort on your right. Soil drainage and the construction of locks and weirs in the Lee valley have reduced the river Stort and Wicken Water to tiny streams but even now a period of rain will soon swell them to become the significant barriers to communication that they undoubtedly were for much of the year in Saxon times. Here by the pub and river are some interesting little houses.

Very soon you leave the houses behind and in 500 yards

CLAVERING

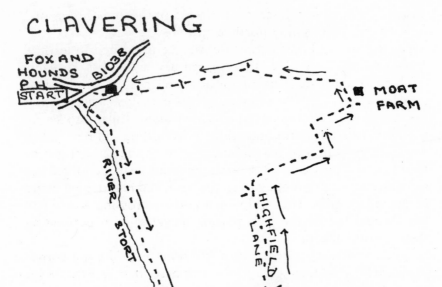

NOT TO SCALE

reach a gate. Pass through along this valley walk. After 700 yards you come to some barns, usually deserted, belonging to Clavering Hall Farm, a few hundred yards to the right by the road. Now reach a lane bridging the river, with the sadly named Poor Bridge.

Turn left and walk up this lane for 600 yards, then at a concrete public byway sign turn left into Highfield Lane which is hedged on both sides. When you come to the junction of three paths be sure to keep on and turn right, walking north-east. This track later takes a sharp left turn then a sharp right down a track lined with trees leading towards Moat Farm.

Just before reaching the farm at the end of the line of trees turn left across a field, going north-west.

Before leaving Moat Farm you may be interested to learn of events which took place there a century ago. Miss Holland, aged 56 and of independent means, met in 1898 Mr Dougal, an ex-army officer whose pension had been lost when he was found guilty of forgery. He persuaded Miss Holland to set up with him in Moat Farm, intending to live off her money. When she took exception to his philandering with the servant girl he shot her, and buried her in a ditch. For four years he forged her signature to receive money from the bank and entertained many of the village girls. The field which you are crossing was where Mr Dougal taught the girls to ride bicycles, even persuading them to ride naked.

When you reach a hedge turn left along it to the top corner of the field. Pass through a gap – near here there is a trig point stone. Follow the path under the power lines. All around you are views of Clavering parish.

The church (St Mary and St Clement) was built in the 14th century in the place of what may have been the castle chapel, during an age of confidence and prosperity. It is placed among the first four churches in north-west Essex, the windows containing some of the finest medieval stained glass, with scenes from the life of St Catherine, the Madonna, the head of Christ crowned with golden thorns and St Cecilia. The masterpiece of craftsmanship is the Jacobean oak pulpit, set on its medieval predecessor, which is carved on each of its seven panels and inlaid with other woods. Near the church stands The Bury, the oldest house in the village. It is now established to be an aisled hall manor dating from the 13th century. This together with the Guildhall and the Old House at Church End are all privately owned.

Turn slightly to the left making a steady descent towards the village. You come to a stile which takes you over a meadow to the car park of the Fox and Hounds.

④ Molehill Green
The Three Horseshoes

At the northernmost end of Takeley parish, Molehill Green boasts a shop, a pub, and a scattering of houses. This charming little pub has a pretty thatched roof, and a very well equipped garden.

The Three Horseshoes utilises the modern licensing acts to the full, hence the opening hours 11am – 11pm Monday to Saturday and on Sunday 12 noon – 3pm and 7pm – 10.30pm. The real ales on draught are Benskins and Tetley Bitter with in addition a guest bitter always available. Taunton Dry Blackthorn is the preferred draught cider. For eating there is a good choice and the food is all home-made. Huffers, steak, roast beef, steak and Guinness pie all sound good; in addition there are daily 'specials' plus the usual sandwiches and ploughman's. As is often the case today this pub has become very adept at producing good food, fairly quickly, at a reasonable price and still purveys good beer and other drinks.

Dogs are not allowed in the pub. Children are most welcome in the garden, especially to enjoy the swings and slides.
Telephone: 01279 870313.

How to get there: From Takeley on the A120, travel north 2¹/₂ miles to Molehill Green. Turn right into the village and you will see the pub on the left.

Parking: At the pub on a gravelly park. Please ask permission to leave your car while you walk.

Length of the walk: 4 miles. OS Landranger map 167 Chelmsford and Harlow (GR 563247).

A very pleasant walk in the environs of a tranquil little village not much changed by modern times, crossing by plank bridge the infant river Roding. The source of the river, which flows south and west to join the Thames at Barking, is just to the north of the village (GR 565248). The Roding is the unifying factor in a most characteristic and attractive valley and gives its name to a group of eight charming villages: Roding prefixed by Beauchamp, Abbess, Leaden, Aythorpe, High, Margaret, Berners, and White. North of White Roding there is the site of what was the ninth Roding – Morell Roding.

The Walk
Turn left on leaving the pub and walk past the Village Stores. At the road corner when the road bends to the left continue down School Lane with its interesting houses. Murrayfield Farm is on the left – perhaps a Scottish connection? Pass a public footpath signpost pointing back to the field on your right and just past Swan Farm the way becomes a track at a public byway sign. Shortly turn right with the track flanked by two hedges. In 150 yards the track turns sharply to the left (where you will rejoin it on your return) but you should continue straight on.

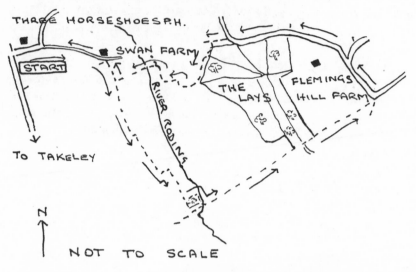

MOLEHILL GREEN

THREE HORSESHOES P.H.

START

SWAN FARM

THE LAYS

FLEMINGS HILL FARM

RIVER RODING

TO TAKELEY

N

NOT TO SCALE

When the hedge on the right ends, bear left and continue with a hedge on your right. When you come to a facing hedge there is unfortunately no bridge at present. What you do is to turn right through a gap in the hedge and immediately left through another gap aiming across the field to the corner of the wood. Turn left along the wood and at the field edge cross over two plank bridges. Now turn right at the side of the wood. When it ends turn right though the hedge to join a substantial track. This is part of the Harcamlow Way from Harlow to Cambridge.

Turn left with this track. Soon come to a crossing farm track where you continue straight on to enter the edge of a wood. Pass through the wood and the track now has a hedge on the left, with a triangular field on the right. As you reach the end of the field bear left through a short tree-lined section to reach a road at a concrete public bridleway signpost. Turn left up the road. Soon you will come to a road junction where you take the left option passing Flemings Hill Farm. Ignore a footpath sign on the right where you join the side of the wood. When the road turns sharply to the right follow a concrete public bridleway signpost past a house, turning left along the wood side on a wide track. Now follow this track around right and left bends to meet the track where you started the walk, at a T-junction.

Turn right and then left past Swan Farm to walk westwards along School Lane. The route which you have taken from the wood was clearly at one time an old road before the times of motor cars. School Lane takes you to the corner of the road where you carry on back to the Three Horseshoes.

5 Great Hallingbury
The Hop Poles

Here near the western boundary of Essex lies Great Halling-bury, bisected by the M11, close to Bishop's Stortford and very close to Stansted airport, yet a more rural parish would be hard to find.

It is known that the manufacture of hop poles was well established in Castle Hedingham to the east when hops were produced in many parts of Essex. Perhaps this also occurred in Bedlar's Green, the part of Great Hallingbury where our pub is situated. At any rate the Hop Poles has long been selected by many out for country pursuits. A few years ago it was closed but thankfully was bought as a freehouse and reopened by its present owner, who now appears to have a thriving business.

Real ales are Old Speckled Hen, Tetley Bitter, and Burton Ale. The draught cider is Olde English. The food is excellent in the Hop Poles – home-made dishes include soup, pâté, beef steak pie and other pies, lasagne, and macaroni, prawns, tuna,

fresh fish, cottage pie. You can phone in advance to book a special dish, and there are daily dishes available. The Hop Poles has a large garden area and children are welcome there but not inside. As far as dogs are concerned they can come in the pub but on a short lead. The landlord has a test that the dogs must be strokable by strangers. Opening hours Monday to Saturday 11am – 3pm and 6pm – 11pm, Sunday 12 noon – 3pm and 7pm – 10.30pm.
   Telephone: 01279 757042.

How to get there: Great Hallingbury lies south of the A120 on a minor road, just to the east of junction 8 of the M11. Bedlar's Green and the Hop Poles will be on the left after a mile.

Parking: Park at the pub. Please make sure you ask the landlord for his permission to leave your car while you go on a short walk.

Length of the walk: 3 miles. OS Landranger map 167 Chelmsford and Harlow (GR 524203).

A peaceful walk in historic Hatfield Forest, once a royal hunting ground. There is much to enjoy, including a tranquil lake and a wealth of bird life, and the walk passes prehistoric Portingbury Hills, now an ancient monument.

The Walk
Outside the Hop Poles turn right and then left along the road for 200 yards. At a road sign follow the direction to a public footpath and continue down The Street. At Hallingbury Street continue straight on ignoring a public footpath sign on your right. Pass the long drive to the Forest House, and bear left along a hedged green lane. Walk through a gate into the confines of Hatfield Forest.
   This is an extensive stretch of uncultivated land, one of the few left in Essex. It is in fact a relic of Essex Forest which

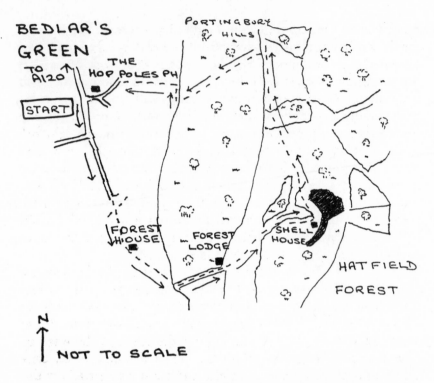

BEDLAR'S GREEN

TO A120

THE HOP POLES PH

START

PORTINGBURY HILLS

FOREST HOUSE

FOREST LODGE

SHELL HOUSE

HATFIELD FOREST

N

NOT TO SCALE

stretched eastwards as far as Colchester. King Harold owned Hatfield Forest and successive kings hunted along the wide rides cleared to give them a better track. Today under the care of the National Trust, walkers are provided with woodland, rides, streams, and an attractive lake. There is also a wealth of bird life including hawfinch, blackcap, garden warbler, jay, snipe, teal, water rail, whitethroat, willow tit, and woodcock.

From the gate into the forest proceed up a wide grassy lane and pass a large house (Forest Lodge). Turn slightly left as you do so. Just after crossing a ditch and hedge line turn right through a wide gap. Ahead there is a magnificent Scots pine and here you turn right towards the Shell House by a large lake. You may want to seek refreshment here at the café.

The lake was created in 1746 when by damming the south end of the Shermore brook, Jacob Houblon covered about 8 acres with water. He built a cottage on the site of the present

Shell House, which was added later that century. Apparently Jacob was beyond his rights in that both the lake and the house curtailed the commoners' rights, yet ever since they have been the focal point for visits to the forest. Shell House was so called because one of its rooms was decorated with shells.

From the café follow the car track north-west. When the track turns sharply to the right follow the posts straight on. After post number 14 bear slightly right through a gate and continue straight on. Turn left along a forest path, soon coming to earthworks. These are called Portingbury Hills, and are traces of what is thought to have been a prehistoric camp, now a scheduled ancient monument. There is a low central mound surrounded by a shallow branch with signs of a larger enclosure beyond. The origin of the camp is a mystery.

Continuing your walk, ignore an arrow to the left but go straight on to cross a broad track. At the edge of the forest when you reach farm buildings turn right for 200 yards to a stile. Observe ahead a large dead twisted oak tree. Now cross the stile to the left and follow the track at the edge of a field with a hedge on your left. When the field ends, turn left to join a track from the right and soon arrive back at the Hop Poles.

You may decide after your walk to visit the village of Great Hallingbury to the south. Hallingbury Park contains the 'big house' with 16th century brickwork. The Parkers lived here for hundreds of years. One was Admiral of the Fleet, another was the 8th Baron Morley who served Henry VIII at his court, but the most famous was William Parker who died in 1622 and is remembered for bringing the Gunpowder Plot to light. In Elizabethan times John Brand's story was recorded in the church archives. One Christmas Eve a devil appeared and showed him plainly where to find Mother Prior's money, which he stole, a sum of £7 18s. Three months later the devil returned and told him better to kill himself than marry the widow he had in mind. John tried with a dagger on Monday, attempted drowning on Wednesday, poison on Sunday. Finally he succeeded in hanging himself.

St Giles', the parish church, has a 15th century tower with thin diagonal buttresses and a tall shingled spire. Inside there is an early Norman chancel made entirely of Roman bricks. A doorway older than Agincourt is still in the porch. A rare feature is the unusually high piscina also of Roman brick. A mile and a half south-west of the church just by the river Stort there is Wallbury, an early Iron Age fort covering 31 acres.

6 Little Dunmow
The Flitch of Bacon

This delightful little inn has been on this site for many years. The present building dates back to the 17th century. What else could it be called but the Flitch of Bacon? In the 12th century the custom started of the Dunmow Flitch, offered to the man who had not repented of his marriage for a year and a day, and who took an oath to that effect before the prior, the monks, and the townsmen of Little Dunmow. The custom survives to this day, and now every four years before a court of six maidens and six bachelors of the parish, married couples swear that they have not quarrelled for a year and a day.

There are usually three real ales, Greene King IPA, Timothy Taylor's Landlord and a guest beer. Scrumpy Jack is the chosen draught cider. The menu has an English theme: Flitch ham on the bone, and three home-made pies, pig in a blanket, steak and kidney, and fish. In winter game dishes are available like venison, pigeon and rabbit. Accommodation can be arranged for there are three double rooms to let. You must visit Little Dunmow for the kind and enthusiastic service you will receive at the Flitch of Bacon. Children can be accommodated in the party room. Dogs are welcomed provided they are well behaved.

Opening hours are Monday to Saturday 12 noon – 3pm and 6pm – 11pm, Sunday 12 noon – 3pm and 7pm – 10.30pm. You may find the pub open a little later on Saturday afternoons. Telephone: 01371 820323.

How to get there: From the A120, take the turning to Little Dunmow and Felsted, just east of Great Dunmow. After ½ mile fork right into the village and the Flitch of Bacon is on your right.

Parking: Park at the pub. The landlord also owns the field opposite.

Length of the walk: 3¼ miles. OS Landranger map 167 Chelmsford and Harlow (GR 656216).

This walk gives fascinating glimpses of the past and country views which can be enjoyed throughout the year. The village of Little Dunmow stands between Roman Stane Street (the A120) to the north and the river Chelmer to the south. Running close by was the Braintree to Bishop's Stortford railway. The disused line has been converted into a linear country park with a waymarked route for walkers, called the Flitch Way.

The Walk

On leaving the pub turn right down the road. There is a very tall water pump painted green, erected for the Victoria Jubilee in 1887. Many of the house names end in 'Barn': Rose Barn, Kings Barn and Barley Barn.

The road bends to the left. When you come to the through road cross over to a concrete public bridleway sign. This points

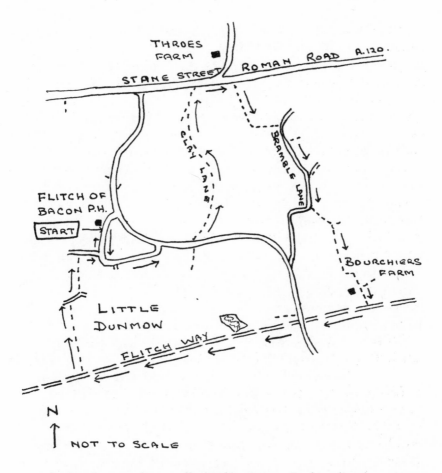

up a hedged green lane called Clay Lane. Such solitude as you walk up is slightly marred by the traffic noise from the A120. This is of course Stane Street, a famous Roman road.

We turn to the right along this passing Throes Farm and soon coming to a concrete public footpath sign. Turn right here following a good farm track. Look back to the left for views of Stebbing church and the village. The track turns left now with a hedge alongside. Now there are views to the right of Felsted church and the school.

We come to Bramble Lane, a quiet road leading south. Ignore the first concrete footpath sign on the left. Later a concrete sign has 'Felsted' attached. Walk along a farm track bearing right towards Bourchiers Farm, passing a pond on your left. At Bourchiers follow the track to the left and then turn right to pass the house. Notice in the garden a lovely yew tree. Right behind the farm is a disused railway line. It has now been renamed the Flitch Way, from Braintree to Bishop's Stortford.

Turn right along this. A sign (Path) invites you to climb some steps up the bank, in order to enjoy the open views to the south, but it is not long before more steps bring you back to the base. Bear left at a wooden fence to descend to the road. Turn right through the remains of a bridge and climb steps to the left by a concrete public footpath sign. Keep to your right at the station and walk by a Flitch Way notice. The path has a hedge on the right. Cross over a wooden bridge and up some steps to the railway line.

Pass under a railway bridge; now you can see to the left the large farmhouse called 'Brick House'. Turn right off the railway at a Flitch Way sign to Little Dunmow. Walk up the field edge with a hedge on your left. At the top of the field keep to the left through a hedged path out to a concrete public footpath sign. Keep on up a track with the churchyard on your right.

The Augustine priory of Little Dunmow was founded in 1106. All that now remains is the south chancel chapel which is used as the parish church, for like many others the priory was destroyed in 1536. The bell turret of the church rests on the masonry which formed the corner stones of the priory's central tower. The font and a beautiful pillar piscina are both 600 years old and there are two coffin lids of the same time. The shafts of the east window come down to the floor. Set into a wall are about a dozen brightly coloured 14th century tiles, on one of which a man and a woman are exchanging rings under a tree.

At another concrete public footpath sign turn right to the road and then left back to the Flitch of Bacon.

7 Hatfield Broad Oak
The Cock

The most famous tree in Hatfield Forest was the Doodle Oak, said to have been 60 feet round at the base. This may well have been the 'broad oak' which gave the neighbouring village, then Hatfield Regis, its ancient nickname. The Benedictine priory was founded in 1135 by the second Aubrey de Vere who also built Hedingham Castle. Though of some importance, the priory was suppressed in 1536 by Henry VIII. Part of the structure of the Cock was originally in the priory, and of course the church was once the nave of the priory church.

The Cock is an excellent place in which to eat or drink. Much of the food is prepared under the watchful eye of the landlord, and no doubt the range and quality of the real ales are his responsibility also. Adnams bitter is an omnipresent and alternatives are Batemans XXXB, Adnams Broadside, Nethergate Old Growler plus guests. Two draught ciders are Scrumpy Jack and Addertones Cask Conditioned. The food, as well as on a menu, also appears on a daily blackboard: sandwiches, Huffers, with ham, cheese, prawns, sausages and bacon, with main courses of smoked lamb, beef, salt beef and chicken.

The rooms are comfortable with a period feel and the garden is nicely situated beside the church. Both children and dogs are free to go in the Cock provided that in each case they are well behaved. This is definitely a place to come back to either for another walk or with a party for a lunch. Opening hours are Monday to Saturday 12 noon – 3pm and 5.30pm – 11pm, Sunday 12 noon – 3pm and 7pm – 10.30pm.

Telephone 01279 718306.

How to get there: Hatfield Broad Oak lies to the south-west of Dunmow. In the centre of Takeley on the A120 turn south on the B183. After about 2½ miles the road turns right along the main street. The Cock is on the right.

Parking: The pub car park is through the buildings coaching-inn style. Please ask permission to leave your car while you walk.

Length of the walk: 5 miles. OS Landranger map 167 Chelmsford and Harlow (GR 546166).

This is a special walk in a special place. Enter the village at half light, when narrow roads and pavements blend into one with silhouettes of uneven pitched roofs and bulging walls of timbered buildings, and it is not difficult to glimpse back to medieval times. Pass through the Cage End part of the village and visit delightful Hatfield Heath. Walk by Lancasters, an impressive house, to find your way back with the church beckoning.

The Walk
Outside the Cock cross and follow the street downhill. Many of these houses are worth a study, in fact the whole village is

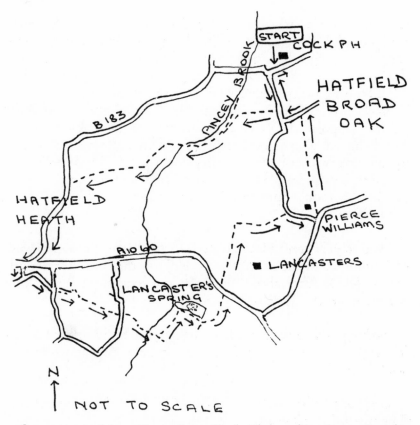

NOT TO SCALE

a fine composition. Pass Cage End Close, then just past the village hall turn right at a concrete public footpath signpost. Pass close to a new building and cross a stile. Follow the track alongside the Pincey Brook.

Just before a facing hedge turn right at a stone with an arrow and the legend FP 23. These stones are to be found all over the Hatfield Broad Oak parish and were the work of Councillor Lumley, who was instrumental in his time in waymarking the paths for the benefit of all walkers. Through the little thicket take the left fork and cross a bridge over the brook. Turn half-left aiming for another stone with white arrows. Take FP 22 over the bridge slightly left to a modern waymark post. This one has already lost its arrows! Turn right with a hedge on your left. Pass a riding school to reach a road, the B183, turning left at a concrete public footpath signpost. The house opposite is unusually called Town Grove.

As you come to the centre of Hatfield Heath walk straight on over the heath, crossing the A1060 with care. At the end of a row of houses on your left where two roads join, pass a house named Lyndhurst and turn left along a green path. Turn left and right with a house on the right and take the left fork through a gap in the hedge. Cross this field aiming to the right of a tree clump and to the left of a farmhouse.

You will come to a gap with a concrete public footpath signpost and cross a farm lane to follow another footpath sign with a hedge on your right. After 200 yards turn right through a gap then left along a broad green track with a hedge on your left. Cross the Pincey Brook over a farm bridge. Turn left along the field edge encouraged by a public footpath sign. At the field corner turn right with a wood now on your left and climb. Past the wood you follow a ditch to the left. There are extensive views including Hatfield Broad Oak church. 'Hill Farm' on the map has become several large residential houses. But an attractive green lane leads you to a concrete public footpath signpost at a road, the A1060. This is busy so cross with care.

A concrete public footpath signpost points downhill through a gap in the hedge. You come to the corner of a wooden fence. Continue over the drive of Lancasters, the fine house to your right, and walk over an earth bridge up a crop division. Almost at the top of the hill turn right along a tractor-marked path to the corner of a hedge. Cross another earth bridge and continue eastwards with a hedge on your left. After passing a house you reach a road at a concrete bridleway sign. Turn right along the road and left at a junction. You soon come to a concrete public footpath sign and turn left through farm buildings, bearing right onto a field.

Continue with a hedge on your left. The church steeple is prominent ahead. The tower is 15th century and is 80 feet high, looking good from a distance and dwarfing the village. It takes the place of a central tower of which some of the piers are still visible – Norman workmanship like most of the north wall. A chapel by this wall was rebuilt in two storeys in the 15th century. The aisle windows were high so that they could look over the cloister roof below.

After crossing a wide ditch continue with the ditch on your right. At the end of the field turn right through a hedge gap and walk on a marked path across the middle of the field out to a road at a concrete public footpath sign. Turn left along the road. At the junction turn right towards trees and beautiful houses before reaching the Cock.

8 Matching Tye
The Fox

The Fox at Matching Tye is quite small and cosy, with a good selection of real ales and tempting pub food. The beers available continually vary but normally there are at least three beers, definitely all worth drinking. The food is certain to satisfy your appetite. It is all home-made so you can try fisherman's pie, steak and kidney pie, or toad in the hole. Dogs can enter the pub, and young children are allowed in the dining room. Opening hours are Monday to Saturday 12 noon – 3pm and 6pm – 11pm, Sunday 12 noon – 3pm and 7pm – 10.30pm.
    Telephone: 01279 731335.

How to get there: Matching Tye lies to the east of Harlow. The nearest 'main' road is the B183. If coming from the A414 turn east along the B183 and turn right after a mile, crossing over the M11, to reach Matching Tye in 1 more mile.

Parking: Park at the pub. The landlord will normally be happy for you to leave your car while you do the walk.

Length of the walk: 3½ miles. OS Landranger map 167 Chelmsford and Harlow (GR 515113).

Matching parish is dispersed over several miles. The original site of the village was at Church Green, but by the year AD 500 Matching Green and Matching Tye had been formed. Matching is one of the gems of Essex, with two greens, a medieval cottage, a lovely gabled house, a 17th century farm across a moat, and the lovely church of St Mary the Virgin. This walk encompasses the sublime beauty of the three Matchings. You will want to stop at the church and the green to savour the settings, as well as enjoy the glorious countryside.

The Walk
From the Fox cross the road and walk past the telephone box by the small village green. Carry on for a few yards bearing left with the road and turn right off the road along a path signposted 'Forest Way', with a hedge on your right. The path continues for ⅔ mile to reach a road and a Forest Way waymark.

Turn right to reach the church at Matching, dating from the 13th century on the site of the original wooden church. The church tower is 15th century, the south aisle wall is 14th century, and the west part of the north and south arcades are 13th century. There are grotesque corbels in the oldest wall, showing two poor people with toothache.

In front there is the Marriage Feast Room. This is timber framed and plastered. It is of great interest because of its purpose rather than its appearance. Mr Chimney of Matching built it in 1480 for the use of local brides for their wedding breakfast. What a good and kindly idea. It was last used for this purpose in 1936 but the privilege remains.

Find a concrete footpath sign and turn right through a kissing-gate. Follow the fence on your right walking past Matching Hall and cross a stile. Now walk across the open

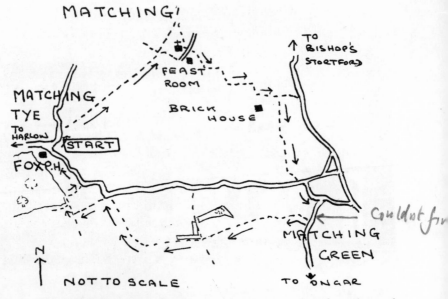

MATCHING

TO BISHOP'S STORTFORD

FEAST ROOM

MATCHING TYE

BRICK HOUSE

TO HARLOW

START

FOX P.H.

Couldn't fu

MATCHING GREEN

N

NOT TO SCALE

TO ONGAR

field, bearing left, towards the Brick House ahead and reach the left-hand edge of the field edge. Keep straight on this edge for about 100 yards and turn left by a waymark along a path between crops. Turn right with this path and close to the house turn left on to a farm drive. The drive crosses a thicket; here turn right with a hedge on the right. About 450 yards ahead you will see a sports field and some houses. This is Matching Green. Augustus John the famous artist was resident in Matching Green. He lived at Elm House next to the Chequers with his wife, children, and mistress. Locals recall that he was disliked because he painted nude ladies, which was definitely not done in those days.

Turn left in the corner of the sports field and look for a gap on the right to take you into a twitten by two houses to the road. Observe the old wooden footpath sign with the legend 'To Matching Church'. Follow the road to Moreton past Lascelles, a very large house. Cut over a little green and follow a road to the right. After 170 yards there is a well obscured concrete public footpath sign by a stile. Here turn right and cross the field on a well marked path. Cross another stile and

House opposite the pub, Matching Tye.

turn right and then left along the field edge with a hedge on your right. At the end of the field the path is slightly obstructed by a fence but this can easily be negotiated.

Now you cross a plank bridge over a ditch. Turn right at the waymark and follow the field edge. At the corner the arrow points straight on and that is where you walk across the open field to the left-hand edge of the wood ahead. Find another waymark and continue on the edge with the wood on the right. When this wood ends cross the field to a small gap between a fence and a wood. Cross a plank bridge. At the end of this wood walk half-right across the field to the hedge corner. Now walk along this edge keeping it on your right.

At the road turn left along the bridleway to reach a post with blue and yellow waymarks. Turn right and just before the wood turn right and left over an earth bridge. Continue with the wood on your left. On reaching a fence turn right. As you reach the road turn left through a gap to a concrete footpath sign. Turn left along the road leading to Matching Tye and soon return to the Fox and your car.

9 Great Waltham
The Beehive

Great Waltham is said to be one of the largest parishes in England. It includes Ford End, Howe Street, North End and Broads Green. Four pubs were listed in 1769 – all are still there.

Born in the 1950s when the original building was demolished to enable road widening, the Beehive occupies a place in the core of the village. The landlord is a tenant to Ridleys Brewery which is only a few miles away at Hartford End. It is an important stop on the Ridley Round, which is a walking route connecting several Ridley pubs, among them Pleshey, North End and Littley Green.

The Beehive has long provided excellent traditional pub food to accompany its fine Essex beers. There are home-made steak and kidney pies and puddings, and regularly a game pie is on offer. What about deep dish Yorkshire puddings with fillings before a country walk? Of course ploughman's or sandwiches are available and on a Sunday you can have a full roast meal. To cater for younger members of your party there is a children's menu, so children are welcome in the restaurant. Not so dogs however, though in bad weather they may be brought into the public bar. Real ales are Ridleys Mild, IPA and ESX, and Strongbow cider is on tap. Opening hours are Monday to Saturday 11.30am – 3pm, and 6pm – 11pm, Sunday 12 noon – 3pm, and 7pm – 10.30pm.

Telephone: 01245 360356.

How to get there: Great Waltham is north of Chelmsford. Take the B1008 to Broomfield, pass a hospital and then turn left to Great Waltham. Just past the church you come to the Beehive on the left.

Parking: Park behind the pub. Please ask for permission to leave your car when you go for your walk.

Length of the walk: 4 miles. OS Landranger map 167 Chelmsford and Harlow (GR 695135).

This walk takes you through peaceful countryside and by the valley of the Walthambury brook, especially lovely in the autumn. The village and church of Great Waltham are a fascination in themselves, the parish boasting over 80 listed buildings to admire.

The Walk
From the pub turn towards the church. This would thrill anyone in love with the old and the beautiful. The tower, nave and chancel were built by the sons of Norman invaders and have stood for more than 800 years. Roman bricks are at the corners of the walls, and Norman windows still give light in the tower, but the building has been filled out and updated so that it now seems a typically large building of the 15th century. Also from that period are the carved pews and the hammer-beam roof with its soaring angels.

45

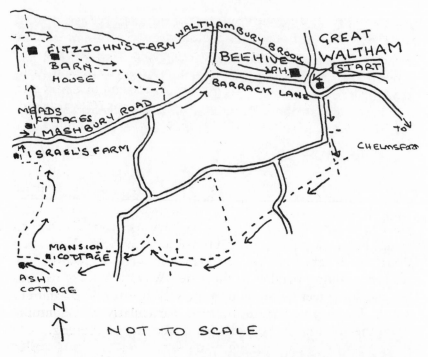

At the main road turn right and right again just past the Six Bells car park. Walk past the village hall on your left and continue with a green on your right. When this road turns right walk between two houses in the corner to a stile. This leads into a field and you walk down the headland path with a hedge on your right. At the end of the field cross over a stream by a plank bridge, taking a curved path into the field on your right.

With the stream now on your right pass South House Farm to reach a concrete public footpath sign by a narrow road. Cross over to another footpath sign and continue on. After 300 yards turn right over an earth bridge and immediately left by a waymark. Ignore a waymark pointing to the left and continue along the field edge. The path at this point has been realigned to the right due to gravel workings, but having veered to the right it turns left back to the original point on the road.

Cross over to a public bridleway sign and go along a broad track for 400 yards to a cottage on the right called Mansion Cottage. Pass some more attractive old houses, and when you reach Ash Cottage turn right along another track and make your way with a hedge on your right. At the end of a field turn left with a ditch now on your left. Turn right for 200 yards then left to Israel's Farm. Go right through the farm buildings to a public bridleway sign at a road.

Now turn right for 130 yards passing a large pond. Turn left at Meads Cottages by a public bridleway sign. You will soon reach a hedge-lined farm road. Arriving at Fitzjohn's Farm keep down the left of the house to reach a broad crossing track. The farmhouse has a 15th century hall roof. Turn right along this track passing Barn House to your right. Now walk along this delightful hedge-lined lane for over 1,000 yards. You are here walking parallel to the Essex Way, 400 yards to your left and some feet below you in the valley of the Walthambury brook. This is a very beautiful spot, particularly in the autumn when the colours of the hedges and trees are so striking.

When you reach a road turn left along it; it is called Mashbury Road. When you come to some houses turn right along Barrack lane. It is only a further 600 yards from here to reach the car park at the Beehive.

Take time to look around the rest of the village before you leave. The village is dominated by Langleys standing in its own park. The owners are the Tuffnel family, who have been here since 1685. The present building dates from 1719. It encases an older building, so preserving some amazing fireplaces and ceilings and some of the most extravagant Jacobean baroque in England. Including Langleys there are more than 80 listed buildings within the parish, a rich heritage from the days of the Tudors, Cromwell, and Charles II.

10 Nazeing
The King Harold's Head

Both the pub and the farm we visit on this walk are named after King Harold who once owned Nazeing (the word Nazinga means headland and meadow). In the King Harold's Head, a comfortable two-bar pub, the real ales are Courage Directors, Ruddles Best Bitter and John Smith's Bitter, with, for cider lovers, Taunton Dry Blackthorn. The food is tempting in this fine pub – steak and kidney pie, steak and Guinness pie, ham, egg and chips, plaice, lasagne, steak, chicken, gammon, duck and trout are on the regular menu, with in addition daily specials on the blackboard. Children are served in the restaurant. Sorry, dogs are not welcome. Opening hours are Monday to Saturday 11.30am – 3pm and 5.30pm – 11pm, Sunday 12 noon – 3pm and 7pm – 10.30pm.
Telephone: 01992 893110.

How to get there: From Waltham Abbey, drive north on

the B194. Fork right at the Coach and Horses public house to arrive at Bumble's Green. Take the second exit off the roundabout and soon arrive at the King Harold's Head.

Parking: Park at the pub. Please ask permission to leave your car while you do the walk.

Length of the walk: 4 miles. OS Landranger map 167 Chelmsford and Harlow (GR 412051).

Nazeing spreads 5 miles over the low hills above the Lea valley. As it is so long, it is divided into Upper Nazeing, Middle Street and Lower Nazeing; Upper Nazeing is at least 100 feet higher than Lower Nazeing. South of Nazeing is an area of quite remarkable remoteness with London so near. A single road connects Nazeing to Upshire, creating a walkers' paradise including 400 acres of Nazeingwood Common. This walk gives you a sample of the wonderful walking area north-west of Epping from the delightfully named hamlet of Bumble's Green, with views over the Lea valley and peaceful woodland to explore.

The Walk
From the pub turn right and walk back along the road until you reach a roundabout. The exit on the left from this roundabout is marked 'No through road'. There is a through passage for walkers and horses and it is here that our walk begins.

Keep straight on when the lane turns right and the way becomes a green lane. At the top of the hill the green lane turns right. At this point there are good views over the valley, Nazeingwood Common and Harlow beyond. Keep your eyes open for a Coal Duty Post on the right of the path. There are 219 posts of this sort surrounding London. They are white painted cast-iron depicting the City of London's ensignia and mark the crossing of the City Coal Tax boundary and entry by road or bridlepath into the Metropolitan police district.

Follow the track round to the right from the top of the hill,

BUMBLE'S GREEN NAZEING

START KING HAROLD'S
HEAD PH

COPY WOOD

TO WALTHAM ABBEY.

HAROLD'S PARK FARM

DEERPARK WOOD

PARVILLS

CLAVERHAMBURY

N

NOT TO SCALE

keeping to the left edge of the wood. Towards the bottom of the hill the wood on the left ends and you pass through a gap into the field corner. Walk diagonally just west of south down to an earth bridge over a ditch. Now go uphill to a stile in the corner of the field. Deerpark Wood which has been on your left since leaving the track is always a beautiful sight, especially in the autumn.

Over the stile turn left (straight on) across a field to another stile. Soon turn right over a bridge then left along a fenced path passing the greyhound kennels. You will come out to a lane at Claverhambury. Turn left here and follow this lane for about 1 mile. The lane becomes more grassy and turns fairly sharply right to go downhill. About ½ mile after the right turn in the lane there is a wide hedged track on the left. Turn up this track and continue for ¾ mile till it leads uphill to become a lane with Parvills Farm ahead to the left. Parvills is a 16th century timber-framed farmhouse.

Pass the farm to turn left over a stile beside a Forest Way sign. Follow along the left edge of the field to cross a stile. You will keep to this visible path past another Forest Way sign over a bridge to cross a stream and then straight up to pick up a hedge on the left. Pause here to savour the views behind you.

Cross a stile on your left continuing your direction on a track and follow the Forest Way signs to a crossing track at Epping Long Green. Turn left along this track and go uphill to a gate on the left leading into a field. Continue with Copy Wood on your right and walk along the right edges of fields. Harold's Park Farm is in full view ahead and there are super views of Broxbourne and Harlow. Pass a pillbox then a pond and, at 103 metres, the high point of the walk marked by a triangulation stone. Onwards now to the farm, turning right between buildings, and soon passing the farmhouse on the right. Continue downhill to the road turning right to the King Harold's Head.

11   Epping Green
The Travellers Friend

The Travellers Friend stands on the corner of the B181 in Epping Green. It is ideally positioned for local walks being right on the line of the 'Long Green' path to east and west. The decor is very attractive, with old brasses and ovens a feature. The pub is a McMullen's house and so AK Original and Country Bitter are on offer together with a guest beer. If you prefer you can have Strongbow cider. The menu is varied, and when you have ordered a large, numbered duck will stand on your table. Those items catching my eye included salt beef sandwiches, tacos (tortillas with fillings), Surf and Turf (sirloin steak and scampi), a variety of omelettes, and treacle pudding. Also there is always something for the vegetarian taste.

Dogs are not permitted in the Travellers Friend. Well behaved children are welcome. Opening hours are Monday to Saturday

11am – 3pm and 6pm – 11pm, Sunday 12 noon – 3pm and 7pm – 10.30pm.
 Telephone: 01992 572462.

How to get there: Epping Green lies to the north of Epping, on the B181. From Epping take either the B182 or B181, which join at Bury Farm. Continue on past Epping Upland church to find the Travellers Friend on a road corner.

Parking: In the pub car park to the right of the building; please ask the landlord if you can leave your car for the duration of your walk.

Length of the walk: 4 miles. OS Landranger map 167 Chelmsford and Harlow (GR 435056).

Epping Green is part of the parish of Epping Upland, in the undulating countryside between Epping and the river Lea. Here the walker finds peace in the most lovely surroundings, where old farmhouses have watched the centuries pass by. This is a fine walk with extended views round many of the historic parts of this parish. Again we find tranquillity only a few miles from Waltham Abbey.

The Walk

To start the walk cross at the corner of the road over to the pond opposite. A selection of ducks are usually to be found either in the water or more often on the grass behind. Walk round the pond to the left, observing the water pump to your left. Cross over a shallow ditch with the help of a plank and enter a narrow path leading to a stile. Now pass through a path flanked by bramble bushes. This leads to a stile and kissing-gate. The path broadens and you have a hedge on your right. When the hedge ends there are allotments and the path bears left to a waymarked stile followed by a plank bridge over a ditch. Continue with a hedge now on your left. Ahead there are fine views of the ridge on which Epping Town is situated.

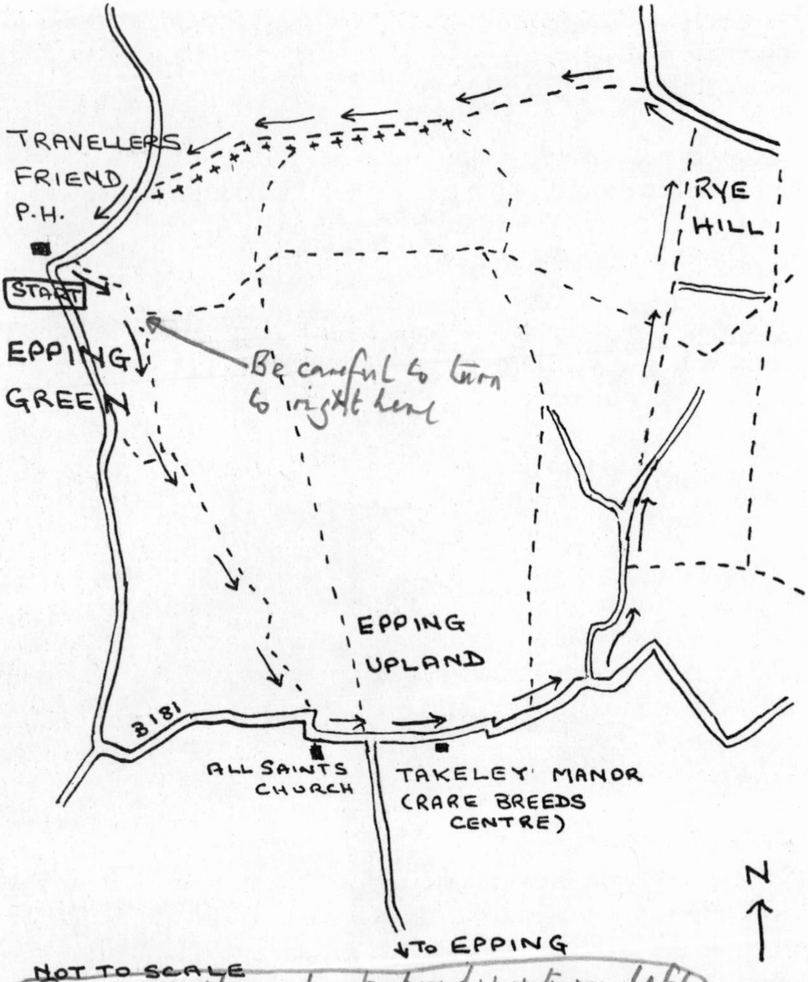

TRAVELLERS FRIEND P.H.

RYE HILL

START

EPPING GREEN

Be careful to turn to right here

EPPING UPLAND

B181

ALL SAINTS CHURCH

TAKELEY MANOR (RARE BREEDS CENTRE)

N

↓ TO EPPING

NOT TO SCALE

Cross another plank bridge + turn left

After 100 yards cross a plank bridge over a ditch – the hedge is now on your right. At the field end cross a plank bridge and go up to steps by a waymark post, turn left along the field edge with a hedge on the left. Now continue on the field edge turning right, left, and right to a stile with waymark and a plank bridge. Turn left by the last field corner and continue through a gap, turning right down a narrow green lane to the road. The stiles and bridges on the walk so far were mostly installed by

Water pump at Epping Green.

Bill Govey's team from the West Essex Ramblers, about ten years ago. That they are still in working order is a tribute to Bill's dedication. His work was valued to the day he died and of course still does him credit.

Follow the road through Epping Upland past the church and Walton, a very large house. The church (All Saints) is 13th century, the tower is 16th century. It has seven bells and is enhanced by a corbel table and a door which is old enough to have a wooden lock. In the church there is a Jacobean chair and a group of Tudor seats. Further corroboration of the age of the church is the nave piscina which is original and clearly Early English. There are memorials to the Colyer family who commissioned James Wyatt, the architect of destruction of so many churches, to build the new Copped Hall. Standing in a park of 400 acres, it was built in white brick and stone, one of the biggest houses in Essex.

Continue on the road signposted to Thornwood. Next pass Takeley Manor with its Rare Breeds Farm centre. Takeley Manor is timber framed, an early 17th century house with an elaborately carved fireplace and floral wall paintings in black and brown on the plaster of an upper room. Along this way are more grand views to the right. Turn left along the first metalled road on the left and follow this with right and left bends to reach Marles Farm cottages. Most of this way is dominated by the impressive sight of Shingle Hall just to your left.

Turn left off the road just before the cottages and walk along a broad track behind the cottages aiming for a clump of trees up ahead. The trees surround a large pond. After passing the pond follow a ditch on your right. When the ditch ends cross the field aiming for a solitary oak tree on the edge of the field ahead. Walk up this edge and finally pass through between houses to a road at Rye Hill. Note the old wooden footpath sign. Turn left past a house named Wayside and soon reach a Forest Way sign. Turn left into a pretty tree-lined track. When the hedge stops on the left continue with a hedge on your right. After passing a barn and farmhouse you're back with two hedges. Next you come to an open space where you carry straight on. Cross another track and join the road at a bend, leading to the Travellers Friend, to the left.

12 Good Easter
The Star

The Star is an attractive post-war building in this lovely village. Once an Ind Coope tied house, it is now operated by Pubmaster with a more liberal beer policy. Four real ales are available, Greene King IPA, Flowers IPA, Bass, and Hancocks HB. If you fancy some cider Taunton Dry Blackthorn is on tap. The food is also tempting, such as home-made steak and kidney pie, oriental prawns wrapped in filo pastry, or sausage, beans and onions, ploughman's, and sandwiches. A small selection of tables and chairs is near the road, and a larger garden behind the pub with bench tables. Walkers and cyclists (and well behaved children) are welcome at the Star and quite often you find friends from the walking fraternity sharing a lunch break in Good Easter. The hours of opening are Monday to Saturday 12 noon – 3pm and 7pm – 11pm, Sunday 12 noon – 3pm and 7pm – 10.30pm.
   Telephone: 01245 231337.

How to get there: Take the A1060 which runs between Hatfield Heath and Chelmsford. At Leaden Roding take the road at a corner, signposted to the Easters; 2 miles onward you arrive at the Star at Good Easter.

Parking: At the pub. Please ask permission to leave your car before setting out on the walk.

Length of the walk: 4 miles. OS Landranger map 167 Chelmsford and Harlow (GR 626122).

Good Easter is a delightful village only half an hour from Chelmsford but still appearing an old-world hamlet. The church spire soars 100 feet above the trees, marking the presence of the village along the valley of the river Can. This walk to Mashbury church and Mashbury Hall returns along the river Can before joining the Essex Way to Good Easter church, through beautiful countryside.

The Walk
On leaving the pub turn right up Mill Lane, passing the old post office. On reaching Tye Green at a public footpath signpost turn right towards houses. Take the left fork to a stile and footpath sign, follow the field edge with a hedge on your left to reach a water treatment area. Walk past this onto a lane. When the lane reaches a road, immediately turn left and left again by a footpath sign and up a field edge to a junction of footpaths. Cross an earth bridge and turn right (east).

At the field corner do not turn right over a bridge but continue over a ditch into the next field. At the end of this field cross over a bridleway and continue with a wood on the right. At the field corner turn left with a ditch on your right. Cross an earth bridge on your right and soon cross right over a wooden bridge. Follow this field edge with a hedge on your left to reach a public footpath signpost at the road.

Turn left along this road, turning left at the corner. In a few yards turn right with a large thicket on your left and follow

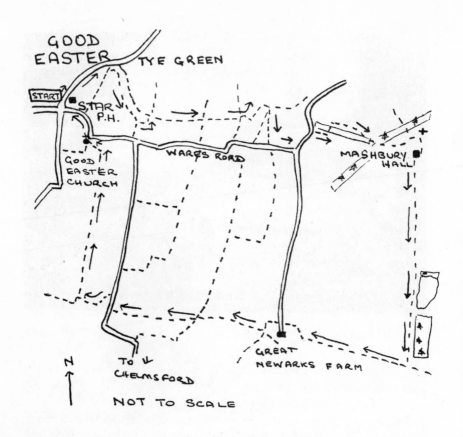

GOOD EASTER TYE GREEN

START

STAR P.H.

GOOD EASTER CHURCH

WARES ROAD

MASHBURY HALL

N

TO CHELMSFORD

GREAT NEWARKS FARM

NOT TO SCALE

this farm track. When the thicket ends turn left with the track bearing right through a wide gap with a large reservoir on your right. Bear left with a paddock on your right and keep to the left of a barn to enter Mashbury churchyard. The tiny church of Mashbury is of Norman times but was altered by the 15th century builders who gave it a new chancel arch and a new east wall.

Turn right at the church and walk towards Mashbury Hall, with a substantial duck pond on your right. On reaching the farm road turn right and follow a garden wall to the left walking through farm buildings towards another reservoir. Follow this attractive path downhill to reach a bridge at the river Can. Do not cross this but turn right along a wide grassy

60

Good Easter church.

pathway between the river and a field. After about 600 yards you will reach a footpath sign pointing diagonally right across the last field before arriving at Great Newarks Farm.

Reaching the end of the diagonal, find a second footpath sign and turn left along the track. Turn left following this track and soon turn right at a public footpath sign walking with a duck pond on your left. Pass through a gap in the fence along a rather rough tree-lined path by the river Can. When you come to an open field keep the hedge on your right for about 100 yards then cross the field towards a white-topped pole and a bridge. Make for the track on your right and follow this with a hedge on your right all the way to a stile and concrete public footpath sign at a road.

Turn right and then turn left at a concrete public footpath sign bearing the Essex Way logo. Walk through a little thicket and follow the field edge. Cross over a bridge and turn right by a ditch. When the ditch ends at an Essex Way footpath sign aim 20 yards to the right of the church steeple ahead, walking across the field. You should arrive at a white-topped post with an arrow pointing across a sloping bridge into the churchyard. In the Middle Ages the church at Good Easter belonged to St Martin's le Grand and Henry VIII gave it to Westminster Abbey. The nave and chancel are of the 13th century and the aisle and its fine arcade are from the 14th century. Though often used as a backdrop to Eastertide, the name of the village is actually derived from Lady Godiva, an early lady of the manor, and 'eowestre' an Old English word meaning sheepfold.

Bear left of the church out to the road and turn left for a few yards to return to the Star.

13   Stapleford Tawney
The Mole Trap

Woodhatch is a hamlet containing just one or two houses, situated in Tawney Common, at the northern end of the parish, and that is where the Mole Trap is located. Despite its remoteness this little pub attracts a good following throughout the year, and when you go there you will see why. Good beer and home-made food, both at good value for money prices, is part of the reason but the friendly reception may count just as much. Until recently the Mole Trap was owned by McMullen's brewery at Hertford, but the sitting tenant has bought the freehold.

Still on offer are Original AK and Country Bitter with in addition a guest beer. The draught cider is Strongbow. The food is fairly simple but jolly good for the money. A typical choice would be – home-made soup, shepherd's pie, ham, egg and chips, chicken curry, ploughman's, and plain or toasted sandwiches, cherry pie and cream, and bread

pudding. Each day there are one or two special dishes which can be ordered. Given that room in this little pub is available, children and dogs are welcomed. Summer opening hours Monday to Saturday, 11am – 3pm and 6pm – 11pm (winter 12 noon – 2.30pm and 7pm – 11pm). All Sundays 12 noon – 3pm and 7pm – 10.30pm.
    Telephone: 01992 522394.

How to get there: Stapleford Tawney is to the south-west of Chipping Ongar. From the A113 take the turning near where the road passes under the M25. This road passes Stapleford Tawney church and $1\frac{1}{2}$ miles later reaches the Mole Trap.

Parking: Park in the pub car park. Please let the landlord know that you are leaving your car while you go for a walk.

Length of the walk: 5 miles. OS Landranger map 167 Chelmsford and Harlow (GR 500014).

Considering that Stapleford Tawney is only $2\frac{1}{2}$ miles from Epping High Street it is a delightfully rural and peaceful place. It is on a hill which runs south down to the river Roding. This is a walk in tranquil surroundings with a sense of the past, especially at Nickerlands Farm and Stapleford Tawney church.

The Walk
After you leave the pub, walk uphill and turn left along a lane. Just beyond a farm yard on the right there is a gate. Regrettably there is no signpost or stile but nevertheless this is the footpath. Through the gate turn left and cross the field to a stile and direction post. A little to the right across the road there is another signpost. Follow this direction across another field aiming to the left of a spiky tree. Don't miss the fine views to your left of Tawney Common as you cross this field.
    Coming to the hedge, locate and cross a metal-railed bridge over a ditch and continue with a hedge on your right. Pass through a gap to reach the remains of Nickerlands Farm on

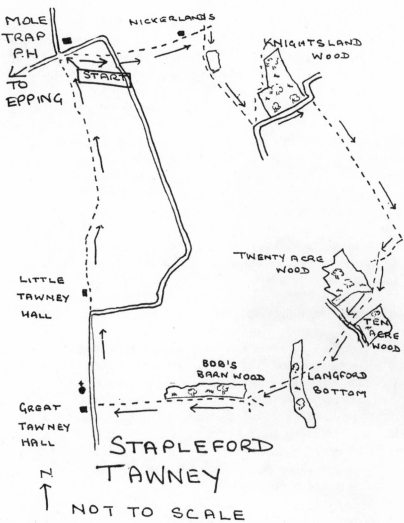

MOLE TRAP P.H

TO EPPING

START

NICKERLANDS

KNIGHTSLAND WOOD

LITTLE TAWNEY HALL

TWENTY ACRE WOOD

TEN ACRE WOOD

GREAT TAWNEY HALL

BOB'S BARN WOOD

LANGFORD BOTTOM

STAPLEFORD
TAWNEY

N

NOT TO SCALE

your left. This area is very reminiscent of farming in bygone days and is worthy of a little exploration. From here a path leads to a broad track (probably an old road but now a green lane). Turn right and cross a bridge, walking up this rough way for nearly ½ mile to come to a bridleway sign and a road.

Turn left along the road with Knightsland Wood on your left. When the road turns sharply left you turn right up a farm

14 Stanford Rivers
The Drill House

The Drill House is another pub which stands proudly by itself. The name refers to a farm drilling machine not the military kind! It lies in the north of Stanford Rivers on the Greensted border. Look for the red Victorian letterbox let into the building. Just a few hundred yards to the north at Drapers Corner, about 200 years ago a man named Draper was hanged for stealing sheep. It is said that his ghost still haunts the corner!

The Drill House is an attractive building with on the left a substantial duck pond and garden. It was very rural 30 years ago when farm animals used to walk through the bar to get to the back! Now it is a smart house indeed, with food and drink to satisfy most tastes. Real ales that are available are Ridleys IPA and Crouch Vale bitter, with in addition a guest beer. The draught cider is Scrumpy Jack. For eating the list is long. Cajun chicken, mixed grill (the big one), lemon chicken, steak, cod, plaice, scampi, Hawaiian gammon, lasagne, jacket potatoes, sandwiches, and ploughman's. If that's not enough there are daily specials on the blackboard! Opening hours are Monday to Saturday 11am – 3pm and 6pm – 11pm, Sunday 12 noon – 3pm and 7pm – 10.30pm. Children are made welcome to eat with the family.

Telephone: 01277 362298.

How to get there: Stanford Rivers lies south-west of Chipping Ongar off the A113. At Little End turn off to Stanford Rivers church. Take the right turn in front of the church and come to the Drill House about a mile after.

Parking: Park at the pub. Before setting out on your walk please ask the landlord's permission to leave your car.

Length of the walk: 3¼ miles. OS Landranger map 167 Chelmsford and Harlow (GR 532023).

Stanford Rivers is a scattering of hamlets, the only 'village' being around the parish church of St Margaret, though Toot Hill and Little End a few miles apart have a separate character of their own. This is a pleasant rural walk in the outskirts of Chipping Ongar, and the return route follows part of the Essex Way and takes you to the famous timber church at Greensted, where worship has continued for 1,300 years.

The Walk
On leaving the Drill House turn right, passing the garden and duck pond, to a concrete footpath sign pointing to the right. Follow this direction along a field edge with a hedge on your right. Cross a ditch and then bear left with the hedge to reach a pond. Beyond the pond cross the earth bridge to your right and continue with the hedge now on your left, turning right at the end of the field to pass Lodge Farm. Watch out for some ponds on the left of the hedge. At the end of the first pond turn left down a narrow path with a second pond on your right.

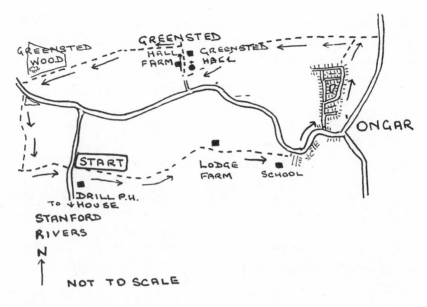

Soon turn right beyond this pond, and then right and left into a hedged track.

Keep on in this direction for over 500 yards to a road by a school. Turn right down this road and take the first road on the left (Fairfield Road). Turn right down Rodney Road which bends to the left. When it turns sharply to the left (west) continue ahead (north) to leave the buildings on a concrete track. This track soon reaches the west/east path between Greensted church and Ongar.

Turn left along this well defined path. Until the arrival of Dutch elm disease this was a glorious avenue perhaps 50 yards wide. It is now reduced to an ordinary field path though boasting fine views of Ongar and beyond. At the end of the field cross the drive leading to Greensted Hall and enter the field opposite. Aim to the left of the church and cross a kissing-gate to the right of a pond. Continue up the drive and then turn right to the church. It is well worth giving this building a visit, it is the oldest timber-built church in Western Europe.

After looking around the church continue downhill through Hall Farm buildings. Turn left with a hedge on your right.

Greensted church.

This route is waymarked as part of the Essex Way. You pass the edge of Greensted Wood. Cross over a road to a footpath sign opposite and walk uphill for about 400 yards to a crossing track. Here the Essex Way goes right but we go left along the field edge for a further 350 yards and out through a thicket to reach the Drill House.

15 Willingale
The Maltsters Arms

Strategically placed at the southern end of Willingale village on the road to Fyfield, the Maltsters Arms has long been a freehouse. Not so many years ago, a change of ownership heralded the development of a restaurant at the rear of the building with a much enhanced menu to go with it.

Willingale is the centre of an excellent footpath network and ramblers have long been welcomed here, even to eat their own sandwiches providing they buy a drink. The policy on beer is to have at least one real ale, but to vary this from time to time. When I was there the chosen one was Ridleys IPA. For lunchtime eating the range of foods includes soup of the day, omelettes, bacon and egg, gammon steak, lemon sole goujons, ploughman's, rolls and sandwiches, ice cream and other desserts. The meals served in the evening are more exotic but of course more expensive. Opening hours

Monday to Saturday 11am – 3pm and 7pm – 11pm. Sunday 12 noon – 3pm and 7pm – 10.30pm.
Telephone: 01277 896245.

How to get there: Willingale lies to the east of Fyfield, off the B184, between Chipping Ongar and Leaden Roding. In the centre of Fyfield turn east past the Queen's Head and then the church, to come after 1½ miles to the Maltsters Arms on your right.

Parking: In the car park behind the pub. Before setting out on the walk please let the person behind the bar know that you are leaving your car.

Length of the walk: 5¼ miles. OS Landranger map 167 Chelmsford and Harlow (GR 597072).

A fine walk firstly through the village and by the delightful hamlet of Miller's Green to follow the river Roding to Fyfield, before walking the Essex Way through the Willingale churches back to the pub.

The Walk
From the pub walk up the main village street passing the famous two churches which formerly represented the parishes Willingale Spain and Willingale Doe. The two parishes have now been amalgamated. Willingale Doe (St Christopher) is large with a great west tower. It has been widely restored though 200 years younger than Willingale Spain (St Andrew), which is a typical Essex church of Norman origin. Originally no doubt these were the villages of rival Norman knights.

Bell House on your right was until a few years ago a pub, and behind the Bell is a thriving cricket club epitomising all the good things in village life. During the Second World War a bomber airfield was constructed at Willingale for the US Airforce, and many attacks were made on the enemy in the period 1943/44. This part of Willingale history can still be

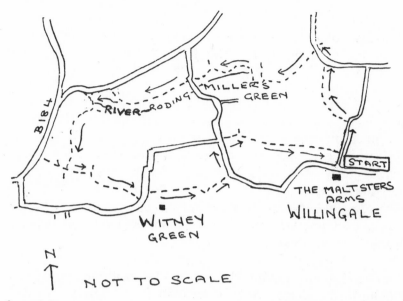

B1894

RIVER RODING

MILLER'S GREEN

START

THE MALTSTERS ARMS

WILLINGALE

WITNEY GREEN

N

NOT TO SCALE

found in remnants of the runway and a number of buildings. Today conflict is restricted to two teams of eleven men on the village cricket field!

Further along just before the road turns to the right, turn left at a concrete footpath signpost, passing between a hedge and a garage then between a ditch and a link fence. Keep the ditch on your left, turning right at the field corner. When you reach a road observe the old farmhouse opposite – Dukes, it is named. Turn left along the road for a few yards and left off the road at a footpath signpost. Keep the property known as Mullion to your right heading round the field edge to reach the fence of a large white house, and in front an expanse of lawn. Turn left and then right following the field edge to exit the field by a gap and a footpath signpost, at Miller's Green.

Cross straight over the little lane by another footpath signpost. At the rear of the house on your right, turn right and follow the field edge. At the corner turn left. Look out for a bridge on your right after 100 yards. Cross this bridge and turn left along a narrow green lane. Soon you come to a wooden bridge which you cross over the river Roding. Walk on for 20 yards and turn left across the field to a stile and public footpath sign at a lane. The path continues straight over the lane but you may prefer to turn left towards the river and follow right, closer to the river bank.

Follow the river for some 1,000 yards to reach a large iron bridge. Cross this and turn right and follow the river now on your right. Come to an old concrete bridge. Do not cross this but turn left following the footpath sign. Soon you reach a crossing track, when you turn right and almost immediately left at another footpath sign pointing up a path with a fence on your left and a conifer hedge on your right. Walk along this long straight path.

When the fir trees end continue along the field edge towards a large white house. There is a gap (the site of an old gate) in the fence which you pass through, walking through the garden with the house on your left and a large pond on your right to a concrete footpath sign by the road. Turn left then shortly right at a concrete footpath sign marked 'Essex Way' at Witney Green. Our route from here to Willingale is on this trail which was opened in 1972.

Turn half-left across the open field aiming just to the right of the church tower ahead to a gap in a hedge beside a waymark post. Now turn slightly left in the direction of the waymark and cross the next field to another waymark post. Pass through a thicket to a road by a public footpath signpost. Turn left along this road for 250 yards. When the road turns sharply to the left walk straight on, soon turning right over a bridge by a public footpath signpost. Turn left and follow the hedge on the left. When you reach a waymark post turn right across the field to a bridge which you cross.

Now you turn left and then right to join a track going uphill with a hedge on your left. Keep up this straight path till you are faced with a fence. Here turn left over a bridge and right towards the churches. Walk right through the churchyard between the churches to a concrete public footpath signpost. On the road turn right to retrace your steps to the Maltsters Arms.

16 Radley Green
The Thatcher's Arms

Radley Green is little more than 4 miles from Chelmsford but has a tucked away in the past feeling, so much so that part of the premises of the Thatcher's Arms is in Highwood parish and part is in Roxwell parish. This is cuckoo you might say and you'd be right for the pub has a nickname – The Cuckoo, though not for that reason. Apparently in the doorway there used to be a stuffed cuckoo in a cage hence the name. In the old days some Blackmore worthies used to walk the 3 miles to the 'Cuckoo' on Christmas Eve, and return home the day after Boxing Day.

Not many pubs are found in the middle of a field, but the Thatcher's Arms is down a drive more than 100 yards from the road. A public footpath runs all that way and then by a stile beside the pub into a field behind. There is a large garden area which is enjoyed on fine days.

Real ales always on draught are Ridleys IPA and ESX, the

latter a somewhat stronger beer. During the year, Ridleys bring out seasonal beers and these will be available at the Thatcher's. The food menu includes soup of the day, cheese or ham ploughman's, beef or chicken curry, vegetable curry, steak and kidney pie, plaice, scampi, lasagne, ice cream sundae, all very good value.

Children are allowed in at lunchtime and early evening, and dogs may come in if well behaved. Having found this secluded and friendly local I hope you will return many times to explore the footpaths around with the help of your map. Opening hours are Monday to Saturday 12 noon – 2pm and 6pm – 11pm, Sunday 12 noon – 3pm and 7pm – 10.30pm. Last food orders are at 1.30pm and 9pm.

Telephone: 01245 248356.

How to get there: Radley Green lies north of the A414 between Ongar and Writtle; 4½ miles east of Ongar look out for a sign to Radley Green. The pub is a few hundred yards down this road.

Parking: In the pub car park. Just let the landlord know that you wish to leave the car while you go for a walk.

Length of the walk: 6½ miles. OS Landranger map 167 Chelmsford and Harlow (GR 622054).

This is a slightly longer walk than most in this book, but is on good surfaces and well worth the effort. Staying mainly in Highwood parish, you skirt Parsons Spring and Barrow Wood. Chalk Hill leads to Loves Green and there is a fine finish along Colley Bridge Lane.

The Walk

Make your way back out of the Thatcher's land and turn right down the lane (Radley Green Road). Pass two footpath signs on the left and reach the end of the lane by Hands Farm. Note the fine old black barn. Cross the A414 with care, bearing right

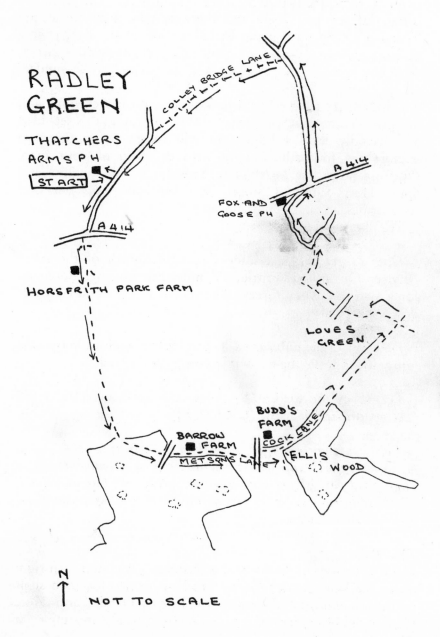

RADLEY GREEN

THATCHERS ARMS PH

START

COLLEY BRIDGE LANE

A 414

FOX AND GOOSE PH

A 414

HORSFRITH PARK FARM

LOVES GREEN

BUDD'S FARM

COCK LANE

BARROW FARM

METSONS LANE

ELLIS WOOD

N

NOT TO SCALE

into the lane by Horsfrith Park Farm at a concrete footpath sign.

Follow this lane (Old Barn Lane) going south to reach two houses remotely placed nearly a mile from the road. Beyond the houses the lane becomes a concrete track and passes through the woods ahead. Your route is to turn left as soon as you reach the woods and follow the edge to reach a road by a concrete footpath sign. Cross the road to a bridleway sign leading to Barrow Farm. Pass the farm and walk this lane (Metsons Lane) through a timber yard to a road. Turn left and soon right down Cock Lane past Budd's Farm. Take the left fork following a bridleway sign close to a house called Elkins. We are now in a very rural setting as the path passes by Ellis Wood on a track known as Chalk Hill.

Leave the wood and continue on the track with a hedge on your left. After a crossing track the path narrows where a barbed fence appears on your right to enclose a vast area for cattle at Writtle Park Farm. When the fence ends cross a plank bridge through a hedge and turn left aiming for a white-topped post. This path follows round the field edge to the point where the deep ditch on your right is bridged by a plank bridge. Cross this and reach the road by way of a garden drive ahead. You are now in Loves Green, part of Highwood parish. Bear right across the road to a bridleway sign by Highwood village hall.

Continue on a good green track. After about 400 yards cross the ditch on your right and walk with a hedge on your left to reach a road on a corner. Turn left down this road to the Fox and Goose. Cross the A414 with care and follow the lane signposted to Cooksmill Green. Ignore a footpath sign on the left (and three on the right). Finally turn left along a green lane at a public byway sign. This is an ancient road from the days before the motor car. It is called Colley Bridge Lane and you emerge into open fields after the bridge. It also marks a constituency boundary. After crossing the bridge continue with a ditch on your right till you arrive at a road. Keep on in the same direction for about 500 yards to get back to the Thatcher's Arms.

17 Edney Common
The Green Man

The Green Man has always had a character all its own, an attractive place with a very large duck pond in the garden. It lies close to the footpaths and bridleways of Writtle Deer Park, but before rushing off to the walk listen to the sustenance on sale, with Charrington IPA or a stronger guest beer, and Taunton Dry Blackthorn cider on draught.

For lunch there are pub snacks, and a good traditional value-for-money daily special, as well as a full roast with all the trimmings on Sunday evenings. Children are welcome to eat if over 14, though in good weather there is plenty of room in the garden. Your dog can go in the pub provided it is well behaved. Opening hours Monday to Saturday 11am – 11pm, Sunday 12noon – 3pm and 7pm – 10.30pm.

Telephone: 01245 248076.

How to get there: If travelling east along the A414 turn right off the road at the Fox and Goose public house set back from the road. Turn left at the T-junction near Loves Green church and the Green Man is ½ mile away. If travelling east along the A12 exit to Margaretting and in the centre of that village turn right (north) over the A12. After 2 miles at a bend turn left into Nathans Lane and at a T-junction turn left to the Green Man.

Parking: There is good parking at the Green Man but please let the landlord know you are leaving your car for 2 hours.

Length of the walk: 4 miles. OS Landranger map 167 Chelmsford and Harlow (GR 649044).

Edney Common and the prettily named Loves Green are the two tiny villages which form part of Highwood parish along the old London coaching road between Writtle and Blackmore. Immediately to the south lies Writtle Deer Park, one-time royal hunting ground, and this is a walk through woods and fields where royal hunting parties used to meet. In the open there are wide clear skies and views sometimes to the north, sometimes to the south.

The Walk
Turn to the left on leaving the Green Man, and after a few yards turn right up a farm road. Two hundred yards further on a white-topped direction indicator points diagonally right across the field. Follow this past a telegraph pole on your left and make for a gap in the hedge by a waymark sign on another white-topped post. Cross a plank bridge and continue over a track to proceed with a barbed wire fence on your left. When I was there a large mixed herd of cattle looked interested as we walkers passed by. A crossing track appears after about 600 yards; your path carries on but on a broader track with the hedge on your right.

Soon you enter the High Woods leading after barely ½ mile to a brush with civilization. At Elkins, a house near Budd's Farm, turn sharp left (there is a concrete footpath sign on the

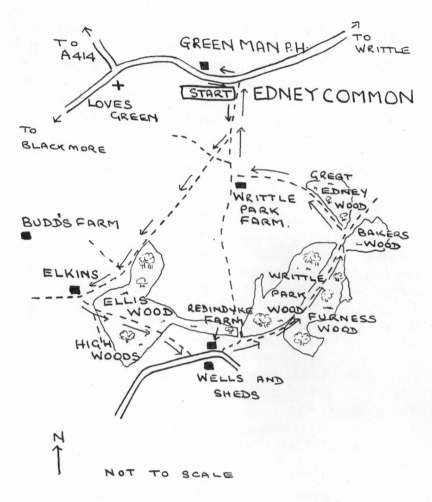

TO
A414

GREEN MAN P.H.

TO
WRITTLE

START ↑ EDNEY COMMON

LOVES
GREEN

TO
BLACKMORE

GREAT
EDNEY
WOOD

WRITTLE
PARK
FARM.

BAKERS
WOOD

BUDD'S FARM

ELKINS

ELLIS
WOOD

REDINDYKE
FARM

WRITTLE
PARK
WOOD

FURNESS
WOOD

HIGH
WOODS

WELLS AND
SHEDS

N

NOT TO SCALE

corner). Now pass three houses to left and right. Continue
uphill to two concrete footpath signs. Follow the first to the left
into a pretty tunnel made by the trees in Ellis Wood. Shortly
this will take you into a coppiced clearing. At this point bear
left a little to pick up a visible path back into the wood.

Soon cross a wooden bridge over a stream. When you see
a home-made footpath sign cross the forest track and by a
butterfly footpath sign enter a narrow path, till you come to
the end of the woods at a plank bridge with a handrail. Now

cross the field aiming for the right edge of the woods opposite. At this point, having spent all of the walk within Chelmsford Borough we are flitting in to and out of Brentwood Borough. Walk down the edge of the woodland and cross a hand-railed plank bridge. Now cross the field very slightly right to a concrete footpath sign by the road. Turn left and walk for some yards past Wells Farm. I much preferred the name on the map ('Wells and Sheds'), however by way of recompense the next farm on the left has reinstated the name Redindyke Farm.

At the road corner turn left at the bridleway sign. Round the corner past a house turn right at the footpath sign and shortly bear right at a waymark. The path uphill which stretches 1,100 yards through the woods is among the prettiest to be found in these parts. True when wet it can be 'wellie country' but at all other times the peace with only birdcalls to be heard is truly wonderful. Eventually you emerge. Stay out of the wood and walk past a white-topped post soon picking up a broad track heading towards Writtle Park Farm. Walk between the farm buildings and a house on your right out to the farm lane. Turn right down this lane for a few minutes soon reaching the road. It's left here for 50 yards to get back to the Green Man.

Spare the time after your visit to the Green Man to visit Writtle Green. Perhaps none of the houses is of outstanding quality, but there is hardly a jarring note in the vicinity of the green, and look for the sight of the church tower peering over the roofs of two picturesque houses.

18 Theydon Bois
The Sixteen String Jack

The Sixteen String Jack is built right onto the pavement and seems to be sheltering in the forest. The pub name comes from the local highwayman John Rann, who was executed in 1774. He was rather a dandy and wore 16 silk strings in his breeches.

It is a McMullen of Hertford house, leased by the present licensees. Here again we have the excellent McMullen's beers, Original AK and Country Bitter. To add to these there are two guest beers which of course vary throughout the year. Strongbow cider is on draught. The food menu is certainly worth a look – hot salt beef, chips and beans, ham, egg and chips, Welsh rarebit, sausage, mash and onions, scampi, cod, prawns, veal, chicken, sausage, egg and chips, and home-made fruit pie. Each day there are specials on a blackboard. If none of this suits you can have sandwiches made to order. Children can be catered for in the Sixteen String Jack, and dogs are allowed if well behaved.

Opening hours are Monday to Thursday 11.30am – 3pm and 6pm – 11pm, Friday and Saturday the same but all day in summer 11am – 11pm. Sunday 12 noon – 3pm and 7pm – 10.30pm.
Telephone: 01992 813182.

How to get there: Theydon Bois lies south of Epping. If driving through the village on the A172 from the direction of the M11, after the church the Sixteen String Jack is on the right.

Parking: Park at the pub. When you want to go on the walk, please ask permission from the landlord to leave your car at the pub.

Length of the walk: 6 miles. OS Landranger map 167 Chelmsford and Harlow (GR 444992).

Theydon Bois is now joined to the City by the Central Line, but it is still an attractive place, on the borders of Epping Forest on one side and segregated by the railway line from the fields to the east. The main attraction is the large green (which is also part of the forest) and the several old cottages standing around. Much of this lovely walk is in and around Epping Forest but there are open sections with views over the Roding valley.

The Walk
Outside the pub turn right and walk up the road for some yards till you soon come to an old wooden footpath sign on the other side of the road. Cross over – the sign reads 'To Loughton'. Follow the drive, ignoring a left fork, to walk through stables. When you reach gates cross over a stile on your right. The path continues on with a fence on your left, and continue ahead when the fence turns left, following the main track round right and left bends till you reach a road at Debden Green.

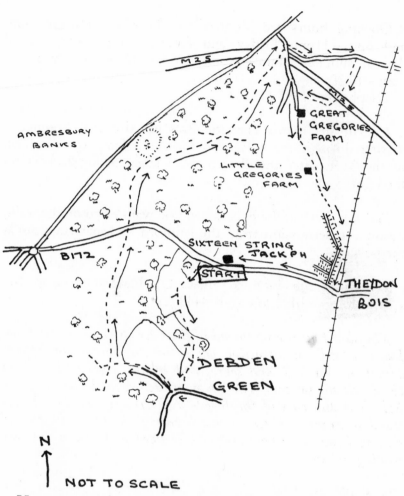

N

↑

NOT TO SCALE

Here turn right and right again to Debden House. Walk straight on up the road to a track in the forest turning left along the edge of the wood. At the top of the hill where the concrete wall ends on your left turn right into a wide track going downhill. Cross a bridge, and now go uphill, then down again to cross a stream in a dip. The path goes uphill again and joins a gravel track from the left. Now follow the main track to reach the road leading from Theydon Bois to the A104. Be careful as you cross over and follow the track round several bends, passing Ambresbury Banks on your left. These are said to be burial mounds from Roman times.

When the track doubles back keep straight on, leaving the gravel track to walk uphill along a fine wide green track. Follow the wide green track to the top of the hill, and bear half-right along a path to a gravel track. Keep right and after a track joins from the right, turn left along a path with a pond on your left. Continue to a road and turn left for 30 yards. When the green on the left ends at some houses, turn right down a signposted track between houses (No 119 is on the right) to reach a road.

Turn left past the Spotted Dog and opposite a school turn right over a stile. Follow on to cross a bridge over the M25. Turn right over a stile with a hedge on your left. Towards the end of the field cross a stile. Follow the yellow arrow up the hill to the left-hand corner of the wall at the top of the hill at Little Gregories.

Cross a stile and walk on to cross another stile into a hedged track leading to a road on the right. Continue along this road into the centre of Theydon Bois. At one time (in the 1920s) the green was the venue for thousands of children from the East End to have a day in the country. They came by bus or long trains – so long that Theydon's platform had to be extended. Sweet shops were open and they even sold sticks of rock with 'Theydon Bois' marked through them. Incidentally 'Bois' – French for wood – is pronounced hereabouts 'Boyce'.

Now walk up the side of the green passing the Queen Victoria pub, the village hall, and the church. The parish church stood in the Roding valley from the Middle Ages, but in 1850 a new building was completed in Coppice Row. It contains two bells from the old church. One of the windows is in memory of Frances Mary Buss who lies in the churchyard. In the 19th century she started a school for girls in Kentish Town and developed a new system which revolutionised methods of teaching. And so back to Sixteen String Jack.

19 Abridge
The Maltsters Arms

The Maltsters Arms has stood at the corner in the centre of Abridge for 400 years. It is a fine weatherboarded building, and having recently been redecorated it presents a proud face to the world. A tenanted house belonging to Greene King, the brewers in Bury St Edmunds, it provides IPA, Abbot Ale, and Rayments for the real ale fraternity. For cider lovers Red Rock is on tap.

Like many other establishments the Maltsters has extended its range of foods available. In the comfortable surroundings of open fires the regular menu is traditional pub fare – various sandwiches, jacket potatoes, sausages, beefburgers, ham and egg, mixed grill. Beyond that there are gammon, chicken Kiev, plaice, cod, scampi, and specials are offered each day on the blackboard. There is a small area behind the pub for outside drinking, however your children are welcome in the bar provided of course that their behaviour is good! Dogs are also allowed in.

The Maltsters is open Monday to Saturday 11.30am – 2.30pm and 6pm – 11pm. Sunday 12 noon – 3pm and 7pm – 10.30 pm. Telephone: 01992 813404.

How to get there: Abridge is signposted at Passingford Bridge on the A113. In the centre of the village on the corner of the famous kink you will find the Maltsters Arms.

Parking: At the pub parking is limited. You may prefer to park in Hoe Lane opposite.

Length of the walk: 5 miles. OS Landranger map 167 Chelmsford and Harlow (GR 466968).

To describe a walk in Abridge is immediately to come under the spell of the legendary Fred Matthews, a long time resident who has championed the walker's cause for many years. Abridge is only a few miles from London, yet this village is set apart in character and style. It has Roman antecedents and is built at a river crossing leading to Theydon Bois. In the course of the walk visits are made to the last remnants of Hainault Forest at Lambourne End and to beautiful Lambourne church. Follow the directions carefully as alterations in footpaths may not be shown on your OS map, and savour the views all around.

The Walk
Step out from the Maltsters with care – London Road is often busy with traffic. Turn right and walk past an ornate log cabin on the other side of the road. It is in fact a café of a good standard. Note the statuettes in the roof. Cross the road and soon reach an old wooden public footpath sign, 'To Gravel Lane'. Walk up a track for just a few yards and cross a stile in the fence on your right.

Now follow the visible path across the field which leads through a gap in the facing hedge. Continue, passing a farm on your right (Great Downs Farm) to a metal gate beside two

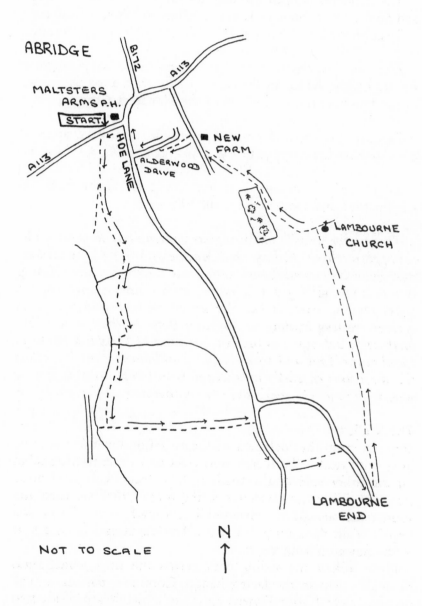

ABRIDGE

MALTSTERS ARMS P.H.

START

B.172

A.113

A.113

HOE LANE

ALDERWOOD DRIVE

NEW FARM

LAMBOURNE CHURCH

LAMBOURNE END

NOT TO SCALE

N

89

white gas markers. Cross a stile and head half-right downhill (just west of due south). Cross diagonally over a field, passing an oak tree in a projecting field corner, to reach a stile a few yards from the bottom corner. Cross the stile and continue down with the hedge on your right to the corner, where you cross a stile. Here be careful. The path was diverted some years ago to follow the hedge to your left all the way to the corner and then to the right down to a waymark on a telegraph post. Walk down two steps to reach and cross a stile and plank bridge. Follow through the field division and enter the next field. The stream is on your right and the path (again diverted) continues for 500 yards. When you spot a stile on your right, turn left uphill to a stile in the hedge, but first admire the views – Chigwell Row church and Hainault Forest to the south, and the Roding valley and Epping to the north.

Now cross the stile and continue east to a junction of fields. Pass right, through a gap, and in a few yards left up a track. From here the footpath should be reinstated to a solitary young sycamore tree. If not continue on the farm track round left and right bends to reach the road. Turn right down this road. At the bottom look for a footpath sign on the left and follow this uphill with a hedge on your left to the hamlet of Lambourne End.

Turn right through the village. At the end turn left at a footpath sign through a narrow path out to a field. Follow this glorious path with views all round; cross a stile, then a kissing-gate. Aim to the left of Lambourne church ahead to reach another kissing-gate and a bridge. Follow the path with a hedge on your right to the church. Lambourne church is a thing of beauty by any standards. The nave and chancel are 12th century, but in the 18th century major alterations were made transforming the interior into that of a Georgian church.

After appreciating the lovely setting of the church turn left for 50 yards and then right through a kissing-gate. Barely 200 yards further turn left at a waymark into the wood and continue downhill to the bottom. The path goes half-left across

Hall opposite Lambourne church.

a field and over a concrete bridge, to proceed diagonally to
the field corner by New Farm. Cross a stile and turn right
past the farm down the track. Turn left at a footpath sign
along the backs of houses. Cross a stile to the right through
to Alderwood Drive. Now turn left to a T-junction opposite
a school on Hoe Lane. Turn right and soon reach the centre
of Abridge and the Maltsters Arms.

20 Navestock Heath
The Plough

Despite occupying a solitary position on Navestock Heath, the Plough has been rejuvenated by its present owner and well deserves its current success for providing excellent beers and wines, and a tempting selection of food. The Plough is a freehouse and has for several years received an award from the Campaign for Real Ale, and a good choice of beers is available, amongst them Brakspear Bitter, Cotleigh Tawny Bitter, Bass, Timothy Taylor's Landlord, Mauldon's White Adder, and King Alfred Bitter.

In the eating stakes there is a wide choice of salads, ploughman's, sandwiches and jacket potatoes if it's a snack you require. There are also home-made soup, lasagne, sausage and egg, ham and egg, chicken Kiev, scampi, fish of the day, and on the blackboard the daily speciality. There is a fine garden at the back and further tables and chairs at the front, and well behaved children and dogs are welcome here.

Opening times are Monday to Saturday 11am – 4pm and 6.30pm – 11pm, Sunday 12noon – 3pm, and 7pm – 10.30pm. Please note there is no food on Sunday evenings.
Telephone: 01277 372296.

How to get there: Navestock Heath is about 4½ miles to the north-west of Brentwood. If you take the A128 from Brentwood towards Ongar, Navestock Side is signposted to the left. Stay on this road, passing Dudbrook and Bois Hall. At the bottom of Ladys Hill, turn right and soon left signposted to Navestock Heath. At the top of the hill turn left on the heath and the Plough is on the left.

Parking: Park at the pub but do ask if you may leave the car before setting out on the walk.

Length of the walk: 6 miles. OS Landranger map 167 Chelmsford and Harlow (GR 539970).

An excellent walk around the Navestock parish, one of the most attractive parts of west Essex, with lovely views over the Roding valley, passing through Navestock Common to the olde worlde atmosphere of Curtismill Green. The walk finishes with a climb from Shonk's Mill by the river Roding up to the heath.

The Walk
After leaving the pub bear left to the end of a hedge. Past the hedge turn left along a farm track towards a small farm. At present you must thread your way through a museum-like collection of old tractors. Pass through the farm and 100 yards beyond turn right along a lane, to continue into a green lane leading to a road. Turn right along the road, and as it bends to the right turn left into the green lane at a public bridleway sign.
The lane continues for ½ mile to a road at Waterhales Farm. Turn right soon crossing over the M25. Pass Watton Farm, with a picturesque house behind a large pond. On reaching

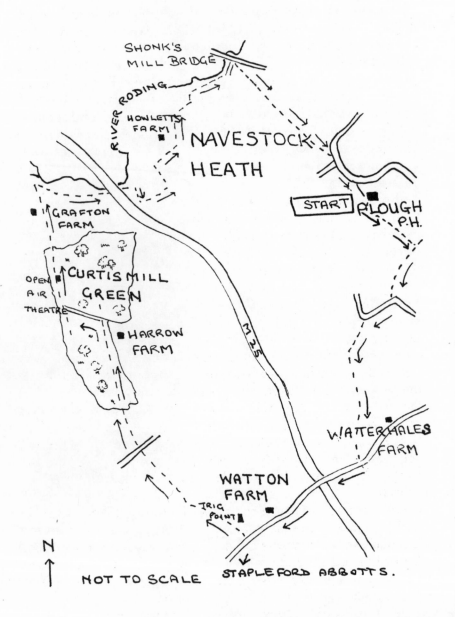

SHONK'S MILL BRIDGE

RIVER RODING

HOWLETTS FARM

NAVESTOCK HEATH

START

PLOUGH P.H.

GRAFTON FARM

CURTIS MILL GREEN

OPEN AIR THEATRE

HARROW FARM

M 25

WATTERHALES FARM

WATTON FARM

TRIG POINT

N

NOT TO SCALE

STAPLEFORD ABBOTTS.

Navestock Common there is a concrete trig point to inspect. Beyond this the byway to the right passes a green gate. Continue with the hedge on your left. After about ½ mile along the byway which has now a golf course on both sides, cross straight over a road to continue on a bridleway. Cross a gravel path bearing to the right and pass by a large house with a tennis court before entering Curtismill Green Wood. Follow the track (north-westerly) crossing a bridge. When Harrow Farm appears on the right, turn left along a stony road. Soon you will reach a clear green space. This is in fact the site of an open air theatre. To your right is the sunken stage. Curtismill is truly a magical part of west Essex.

In the Domesday book Navestock is mentioned as having three manors, and woods sufficient to feed 900 pigs. Curtismill Green is part of the old forest and is in fact the edge of the royal forest. It was allotted as common to the villagers in 1858, having been enclosed by the lord of the manor in 1776, and this right has been re-registered in present times. Water was supplied from the public hand pump until the 1950s and all lighting was by oil till that time.

When the road passes on through the wood turn right, and you walk again in a north-westerly direction. At the bottom of the wood turn right along the first metalled road. Turn left to go under the M25 by the river Roding. Follow the track to the right and left past Howletts Farm and on to Shonk's Mill. At a public footpath sign climb into the field and head uphill towards a bushy tree at the right-hand end of the facing hedge. To your left is a fine view of Navestock church.

On reaching the hedge cross into the next field and continue with the hedge line on your right. At the next hedge corner aim diagonally left across the field towards the red roofs ahead. You will reach a road by a public footpath sign at the end of the field. Turn right to the heath and then make your way back to the Plough.

After the walk a short journey brings you to the church, in a classic position on a wooded hill overlooking the Roding.

Open air theatre, Curtismill Green.

The medieval tower timbers withstood the blast in 1940 of the explosion of a land mine caught in the surrounding trees. The church was rededicated in 1955, not just a patched-up ruin, but a re-creation imaginatively achieved, matching the old with good new craftsmanship.